Paul Groves John Griffin Nigel Grimshaw

steps

TO GCSE LITERATURE

Contents

About this book

The book helps you understand more clearly and appreciate more deeply texts that are the most popular choices for GCSE coursework and examinations.

Every piece you write for GCSE Literature must be clearly a response to the text – it must show that you have understood and appreciated some aspect of the book you are studying.

But this still leaves you a variety of opportunities, from writing about a particular character to adding a piece of your own in the style of the author.

Try all of the methods recommended for the book or books of your choice. Only by doing so will you discover your own best way of showing your understanding of what you have read.

You are encouraged to discuss aspects of your chosen books in pairs or in small groups, to study photographs and critics' reviews, act out particular scenes and make judgements about your own progress. You will probably not be reading all the texts in the book, but do not limit yourself to those you have chosen for detailed study. Use the others for wider reading; each text contains recommendations for others that you could usefully read as companion pieces. Many of the texts could be linked together by a common theme (see the example on page 173).

You should attempt the poetry project. Once you have understood the method, you can substitute poems you have discovered for yourself for any in the project that are not to your liking.

Finally, remember that these recommendations for study are not a substitute for a careful reading of your texts. Read thoroughly first and form preliminary ideas of your own. You will then be able to respond to the suggested methods of approach with a much greater understanding and confidence.

1

Of Mice and Men

John Steinbeck

The background to the book

Of Mice and Men* was written in 1936, the time of the Great Depression in America, when millions of Americans were tramping vast distances, like Lennie and George, from state to state looking for work – any work for almost any wages. The Depression is reflected in the story; in the distance Lennie and George have travelled, in the workers' fear that the boss will sack them, in the hopeless dreams of independence that keep most of the characters going.

A piece of research in your library on the Depression would be a useful addition to your work on *Of Mice and Men*, especially if you linked the details to incidents and characters in the story.

However, *Of Mice and Men* is not about the Depression; if it had been it would not have retained its popularity. It is about people, the good and bad, the strong and the weak, the simple and the cunning. Any background material will help you understand more clearly some details of the story, but it is not a substitute for understanding the characters as individuals, whose thoughts and feelings are those of people at all times, not particular people in a particular setting.

* *Note: Of Mice and Men* is given more detailed treatment than other books to include examples of pupils' work to assess.

Know the characters

Before you write, talk about, or even argue about *Of Mice and Men*, you need to know the characters and the story. The best way to understand the characters is to write down what they do, what they say, and what other characters say about them.

Learning about Lennie

On the opposite page is a drawing of Lennie accompanied by a series of quotations from the book which will help you to think and draw conclusions about his character. In small groups, or as a class, see if you can remember where in the book each quotation is taken from and who said it. Decide what each one shows about Lennie. Look up any you are not sure of. Add any important ones that you think have been missed.

'He was so scart he couldn't let go of that dress.'

'But - Jesus! He ain't hardly got no han' left.'

'If you don't want me, you've only jis' got to say so, and I'll go off in those hills.'

'All the time he done bad things, but he never done one of 'em mean.'

I don't like this place, George. This ain't no good place. I wanna get outa here.'

'Yougonna get me in trouble jus' like George says you will Vou don't do that.'

'You're nuts,' she said, 'But you're a kinda nice fella. Jus' like a big baby.'

'Jesus Christ, Lennie! You can't remember nothing that happens, but you remember every word that I say.'

'He pinched their heads a little and then they was dead.'

'I...I... ain't gonna say nothin'.'

Because ... because I got you to look after me and you got me to look after you.'

'Guy's don't need no sense to be a nice fella.'

'You ask him right away, George, so he won't kill no more of 'em.'

'Make um let me alone, George.'

He pushed himself back, drew up his knees, embraced them, looked over to George to see whether he had it just right.

'He damn near killed his partner ... I never seen such a strong guy.'

His fingers snapped sharply and at the sound Lennie laid the mouse in his hand.

'I tol' you and tol' you.. Min' George because he's such a nice fella an' good to you.'

'This ain't no bad thing like I got to go hide in the brush.'

'Blubberin' like a baby! Jesus Christ! A big guy like you.'

'You ain't fit to lick the boots of no rabbit.'

Learning about George

Reproduce the drawing of George and add quotations about him, still working in groups. You will have noticed that some of the quotations about Lennie also tell you about George. You may use the important ones to add to your list for George. Use some of these quotations to start you off.

'God a'mighty, if I was alone I could live so easy.'

'Think I'd let you carry your own workcard?'

'Don't tell nobody about it. Jus' us three an' nobody else. They liable to can us so we can't make no stake.'

'I'm scared. You gonna have trouble with that Curley guy.'

'You was pokin' your big ears into our business.'

'They ain't got nothin' to look ahead to.'

'No, Lennie, I ain't mad. I never been mad an' I ain't now. That's a thing I want ya to know.'

Add some comments that other people make about George, including the author.

Choose another character

Choose one of the other characters, draw him (or her) and insert ten important quotations round the drawing.

Quotations

Once you have understood the characters, you will be able to identify references to them, even if you have forgotten the actual detail in the book.

Try this with the twenty references below. Each is said by one of these five characters: Curley, Candy, Crooks, Curley's wife, Slim.

List each quotation under its correct character. There are four references for each.

'Why can't I talk to you? I never get to talk to nobody. I get awful lonely.'

'Come on ya big bastard. Get up on your feet. No son of a bitch is gonna laugh at me. I'll show ya who's yella.'

'You hadda, George. I swear you hadda. Come on with me.'

'When you see 'um don't give 'im no chance. Shoot for his guts. That'll double 'im over.'

'You got no right to be in my room. This here's my room. Nobody got any rights in here but me.'

'Curley – maybe you better stay here with your wife.'

'I'm jus' tryin' to tell you I didn't mean nothing. I jus' thought you might of saw her.'

'You god-damn tramp. You done it, didn't you?'

'Well, nex' time you answer when you're spoke to.'

'When they had them previous I coulda went to them, an' spoke in the radio.'

'I been around him so much I never notice how he stinks.'

'You guys is just kiddin' yourself. You'll talk about it a hell of a lot, but you won't get no land.'

'S'pose I went in with you guys. Tha's three hundred an fifty bucks I'd put in.'

'I never got that letter. I always thought my ol' lady stole it.'

'It wasn't nothing. You guys comin' in an' sittin' made me forget. What she says is true.'

'He's scared Curley'll get mad. Well, Curley got his arm in a sling – an' if Curley gets tough, you can break his other han'.'

'Yeah? An' where's George now? In town in a whore house. That's where your money's going.'

'I didn't hear nothing you guys was saying. A guy on a ranch don't never listen nor he don't ask no questions.'

'Candy, you can have any one of them pups you want.'

'He ain't mean. I can tell a mean guy a mile off.'

Add to the references for each character. Use the sketch and labelling method if you wish – it helps you to see the most important points about a character all set out on one page.

How are the characters like each other?

There are strong differences between the characters in *Of Mice and Men*. For example, there seems to be little in common between Candy and Curley's wife. But there are also strong similarities. Look at the references that follow. See if you can remember (if you can't, then look them up) who said each one and in what circumstances. What common theme links each of these characters together?

'You're all scared of each other, that's what. Ever' one of you's scared the rest is goin' to get something on you.'

His eyes blinded with tears and he turned and went weakly out of the barn and he rubbed his bristly whiskers with his wrist stump.

'Guys like us, that work on ranches, are the loneliest guys in the world.'

'A guy goes nuts if he ain't got nobody. Don't make no difference who the guy is, long as he's with ya'.'

'Ain't many guys travel around together, I don't know why. Maybe ever'body in the whole damn world is scared of each other.'

'There wasn't another coloured family for miles around. And now there ain't a coloured man on this ranch an' there's jus' one family in Soledad.'

'Well, I never seen one guy take so much trouble for another guy, I just like to know what your interest is.'

How do the characters cope with being lonely?

Connected with the characters' loneliness are their hopes for the future. Find these references. What have the characters' hopes in common? Decide whether they really believe their dreams might come true.

'An' if a fren' came along, why we'd have an extra bunk, and we'd say, "Why don't you spen' the night?" An' by God he would.'

'An' I got you. We got each other, that's what, that gives a hoot in hell about us.'

'If you . . . guys would want a hand to work for nothing – just his keep, why I'd come an' lend a hand.'

They all sat still, all bemused by the beauty of the thing, each mind was popped into the future when this lovely thing should come about.

'I seen guys nearly crazy with loneliness for land.'

'I tell ya I could of went with shows. Not jus' one, neither. An' a guy tol' me he could put me in the pitchers.'

'We gotta a house and chickens an' fruit trees an' a place a hundred times prettier than this. An' we got fren's, that's what we got.'

Role play

Choose people to take the roles of George, Curley, Candy, Crooks, Curley's wife, Slim and Carlson.

The rest of the class then interviews them about their feelings at certain times in the novel. Not all the characters will be interviewed at the same time.

Below are incidents you might use, together with the characters who could be questioned about them.

Try to respond to the questions as you think the characters would. The interviews should be thought of as taking place some time after the events, but the characters' strong feelings about them would remain. Points have been listed to help you shape the questions.

1 *The shooting of Candy's dog* (George, Slim, Carlson, Candy)
The questioners find out what happened and whether Carlson's shooting the dog was right.
Candy might have changed his view slightly.
Carlson is the person who needs to justify himself most, although Slim could have stopped the shooting. Why didn't he? Ask George what his feelings were. He suddenly started to tell an irrelevant tale about a man with an Airedale dog in Weed. Ask why he did this.

2 *The crushing of Curley's hand* (Curley, Slim, George, Candy)
You'll need to question Curley and Slim in particular about the events leading up to this. Try to establish exactly what happened and why. Ask Curley why he attacked Lennie, for instance. Ask George why he didn't pull Curley away instead of telling Lennie to get him. Didn't he know what was going to happen? Did he want Curley damaged?

3 *The visit to Crooks' room* (Candy, Crooks, Curley's wife)
Everybody should look at this part of the book again before this interview. There is a great deal of suspicion, dislike, even hate;

look, for instance at the vicious talk between Candy's wife and Curley. How does Curley's wife threaten Crooks? Try to ask questions that discover the reasons for the many cruel remarks that are made.

4 *The death of Lennie* (Slim, George, Carlson, Curley)
The last few lines of the book show the contrasting feelings of Slim and George on the one hand and Curley and Carlson on the other. The questions should first establish what happened (George may be forced to admit to his lie about Carlson's luger) and then each character should be questioned about his feelings about Lennie's death. Was it justice? Was it for the best? What alternatives were there?

Write about the photograph

Write about twenty lines to go with this photograph from the film version of *Of Mice and Men*.

Assessing coursework

In this section you are asked to examine pieces of coursework written by pupils doing their GCSE courses. After you have criticised them (which means looking for the good as well as the bad points) you will be asked to try similar assignments for yourself.

Look at the two essays which follow. They are an attempt to write Candy's reminiscences of the time George and Lennie were at the ranch. The students were told to write about the events of the novel from Candy's point of view.

Candy's point of view of George and Lennie

The first time I see that George and Lennie they were swell. They both wore black shapeless hats and denims. One of them was small, quick and dark in the face. The other was his opposite he was huge was that Lennie. I remember those two well because on their first day they were late and I showed them the bunk house. I left them in there and I was outside the door listening to what they were saying I never heard anything but then George came to the door and acused me of listening to them but I got out of it by saying I was scratching my dog and that poor things gone now.

I remember those guys because they were my only way out of this place because we all had a dream about getting some rabbits and a plot of land and we would have a little bungalow and all live off the fat of the land. We had about five hundred bucks between us and George said we could swinga for that.

But it is because of some lousy tart that we have not got it and I am still at this place. That poor bastard Lennie was made to suffer because of some lousy tart. What happened was George went to town and Lennie and I were left on the ranch and Lennie was out in the barn with his pup and Curley's wife went in there and she must of pestered Lennie because he broke her neck and left her lying dead hidden under some hay in the barn and we found her dead. Lennie knew what he had done because he left to hide and he stole Carlson's lugar. They all set of looking for Lennie and they found him or at least George found him they would of shot him straight in the guts so then George came back to the ranch and told me he was dead and I asked him about the land and he said no I guessed it was all talk all the way along.

So you wanna know about George and Lennie

Hi, I'm Candy, I wanna tell you about two guys I used to know. I ain't gonna see em again, I shouldn't think. Well I knows I ain't never seeing Lennie again.

But first I gonna tell ya about George ya see he's always had a dream just he's never got round to it, nor never will I guess. George could never keep his money for long, he'd always go an' spend it, in some crazy whore house. He hopes to settle down in a small house and live on the fat of the land. I know hows I' remember George, he never stopped Bitching, saying stuff like you crazy Bastard and you God damned son of a Bitch. He's always was Bitching at Lennie, not ever anyone else. I means he never meant it to do any wrong to Lennie, I guess, it was just what he liked to call him.

Lennie he was kinda different, strange, wierd, but don't get me wrong he never meant no harm, it's just he never knew what he was doing. Ya see he was always nervous, slow I guess. Lennie had a craz' about soft things, anythin soft he gotta hold of, he'd never let go of it. That's the reason why I ain't gonna see him again. One day he was talkin to Curley's wife. I donna what happened but I know that he killed her somehow. Ya see we found Curley's wife dead in the old barn, me an' George I mean. I guess we knew it had to be Lennie, who else? He couldn't of gone far.

Curley would of killed him if George hadn't found him first. Although George killed him anyway. I guess it was for the best.

George will really miss him, so will I. At least George won' have to care for him anymore, I guess he'll be kinda lonely without him, maybe George will get his dream now to have a small house and live on the fatta the land. I don't think he will, he'll go spend all his money on those crazy whore houses. I hope I'll sees him again, I guess I will

Well that's about it, It's a kinda sad story don't you think so?

Discussion

1 What signs are there that the writers have either remembered, or troubled to look up, actual details from the book? Look particularly for minor details; everyone knows that Candy's dog was shot, for instance; but that Candy said he was scratching his dog when George caught him at the door is a sign that the writer is able to recall less important details. Using such details in your writing is probably a sign that you have enjoyed the book; it also helps to show your understanding of the characters. Are there any of these details that the writers have not remembered accurately?

2 Both writers have tried to see the events from Candy's point of view. What feelings towards George, Lennie and Curley's wife does each think Candy would have? Do you think they have gauged these feelings correctly? Consider, for example, the last thing Candy says:

> 'Candy squatted down in the hay and watched the face of Curley's wife. "Poor bastard," he said softly.'

Who does he mean? Curley's wife or Lennie? Perhaps Candy's feelings about Curley's wife change at the end. Should the writers have included more of Candy's feelings about his dog and about Curley? Do they make enough of the meeting in Crooks' room? Do they stress enough Candy's bitter disappointment at the destruction of his dream? Remember that when George confirms his worst fears, Candy's 'eyes blinded with tears and he turned and went weakly out of the barn'.

3 Both writers have tried to reproduce the language and the method of speaking. How far do you think they have succeeded? Are there any expressions that are not typical of Candy?

4 Examine both pieces for accuracy of spelling and punctuation.

Write about any two characters

Try this exercise yourself using any two characters. As a unit, your work would be better if you chose two contrasting characters, for example, George and Curley, so that you could show differing accounts of the same events. The crushing of Curley's hand would, for instance, be seen very differently by George and Curley.

The next piece of coursework is a very different method of writing about the characters. Read it and consider the questions. The student was given the following assignment: 'Of Mice and Men is a book about loneliness.' How far do you agree?

The loneliest guys in the world

'Guys like us, that work on ranches, are the loneliest guys in the world.'

This statement from George indicates that the characters in this book suffer from loneliness and are aware of their problem. Throughout the book we see the evidence of this from most of the characters and the different ways they compensate for or cover up their loneliness.

With the exception of Slim, all the characters suffer from loneliness, but in different degrees. Probably the most lonely characters are Candy and Crooks.

Candy and Crooks have a lot in common – they are both old, crippled and suffer from isolation, but they still keep their distance from each other for the simple reason that Crooks is black.

Although Crooks would like some company, he knows he is isolated and 'he kept his distance and demanded that other people keep theirs.' He is a very proud man and this statement suggests he ignores others before he can be ignored.

Candy had his dog as a companion but he reluctantly consented to its being shot for its own good as it was old and suffering. Candy had complained, 'I had 'im too long,' 'I had 'im from a pup,' and 'I'm so used to 'im', suggesting that life wouldn't be the same without it, even though the dog would be better off dead. Candy then tried to make friends with George and Lennie as a substitute for his dog and shared in their dream of a home of their own.

Curley, who has no real friends, also suffers from loneliness, which he compensates for by using his power and ferocity. When he first met George and Lennie 'his arms gradually bent at the elbows and his hands closed into fists.'

Here, adopting a boxing stance, Curley threatens George and Lennie and tries to show his power and assert his authority, but reveals the insecurity of isolation.

His wife has both a husband and a father-in-law and is one of few on the ranch to have an official relationship, yet this makes her even more lonely as Curley forbids her to talk to other men. She tells Lennie, 'I get lonely,' 'You can talk to people, but I can't talk to nobody but Curley. Else he gets mad.'

In this case her loneliness leads to her tragic death. She found she could talk at Lennie in the knowledge that he would neither make fun of her film star ambitions nor pass on what she had said as gossip. He is a safe audience for her loneliness; however, her desperation to make contact with someone leads to her death.

George and Lennie both suffer from the fear of loneliness. Lennie's relationship with George only brings about his fear that George will leave him. Lennie depends totally on George and so tries to cement their relationship by an instinctive blackmail.

'If you don' want me, I can go off in the hills an' find a cave. I can go away any time.'

George constantly reproaches Lennie saying that without him, he could play cards, shoot pool, get a gallon of whiskey and spend his fifty bucks in town at the end of every month. But a little later, George defines this kind of life as the only outlet for 'the loneliest guys in the world.' Without Lennie, he would be one of those who 'ain't got nothing to look ahead to.' In fact, in an odd way, Lennie is his inspiration. He tells Candy after Lennie has wrecked their plans by killing Curley's wife, 'He usta like to hear about it so much I got to thinking maybe we would.' With Lennie's death George's hope of avoiding the loneliest life in the world dies too.

Probably the least lonely character in the book is Slim. He is at peace with himself and enjoys his own company. He has great authority, 'the Prince of the ranch,' he is always calm and there is a 'gravity in his manner and a quiet so profound that all talk stopped when he spoke.' Slim is respected and even admired by the other men on the ranch and he is less alone than the others as he is self-sufficient.

As he does for Curley's wife, Lennie provides audiences for other characters and he is perfect to talk at as all he thinks about are his rabbits. We can measure how lonely the characters are by their conversations with Lennie.

Most of the characters in the book have a fantasy. George, Lennie and later Curley and Crooks share the dream of a home of their own. These characters live on their fantasies and would have nothing to live for without them. All fantasies relate to being popular and being with others as all these characters fear loneliness.

With the exception of Slim, the characters in 'Of Mice and Men' all suffer from loneliness, mainly owing to poverty and lack of family to support them. They show their loneliness in their efforts to cover it up and in their hopeless dreams.

Discussion

As with other pieces of work, this also mentions details in the text. In this type of writing, though, it is done through quotation. The method is to give your opinion of the characters and to back this up with details from the book. Discuss in small groups the following statements made in the essay. Decide if you agree with each and see if you can find other details that support or contradict it.

1 Slim is the only character who isn't lonely.
(Whether you agree or not, you almost certainly decide that Slim is different from all the other characters. Start by deciding how and why Slim is different.)

2 Candy and Crooks are the most isolated characters in the book.
(Again decide what is different about them. Do you agree that it is because Crooks is black that they are not friendly with each other?)

3 Curley is aggressive because he is isolated – nobody likes him.
(Is there anything good that can be said of Curley? Is he the nastiest character in the book?)

4 It is Curley's wife's loneliness that makes her behave as she does and it causes her death.

5 George really needed Lennie to give him hope that he could avoid being like other farm-workers.
(Decide whether it is guilt or fear that stops George leaving Lennie.)

6 All the dreams of the characters are connected with having friends and being popular.

Write an essay

Try this type of essay with this title: 'All the suffering in *Of Mice and Men* is undeserved.' (Lennie, George, Candy, Crooks, Curley and Curley's wife are all basically unhappy. Decide how far it is their own fault. Find details from the book to support your conclusions.)

Looking at the plot

Once you have understood the characters in *Of Mice and Men* there is an inevitability about the line the story will take. You don't know exactly what will happen but you feel all the way through that Lennie will be involved in some kind of trouble from which he and George cannot escape. Look at these quotations from the book.

'Look, Lennie. I want you to look around here. You can remember this place, can't you . . . if you jus' happen to get into trouble like you always done before, I want you to come right here an' hide in the brush.'

'Look, Lennie! This here ain't no set-up. I'm scared. You gonna have trouble with that Curley guy.'

'She's gonna make a mess. They's gonna be a bad mess about her.'

'I should of knew. I guess maybe way back in my head I did.'

George not only expects trouble, he knows the quarter it's coming from – a combination of Lennie, Curley and Curley's wife. The reader has only to remember what happened in Weed, and Curley's hand, to be able to guess how the trouble will occur. Remember George had to hit Lennie with a piece of fence in Weed and needed Slim's help to make him let go of Curley's hand.

Changing the story

Write an alternative to chapter 5. The result must be the same – Lennie does 'a bad thing' and has to hide in the brush – but the process could be different. Think about these suggestions; you need not use any of them.

1 It could be Curley who is killed instead of Curley's wife. How could this happen? You could still start with conversation in the barn between Lennie and Curley's wife.

2 Involve the puppies more directly in the climax. Remember how desperate Lennie is to keep one; how would he react if he hadn't killed his puppy and it was taken from him?

3 Perhaps the climax could come with a violent quarrel between Curley and his wife. Might she need Lennie's protection? How could that cause a tragic accident?

Use what you have learnt about the people to make sure they act in character. Try to imitate the language each uses in any conversation you use.

Discussion

Charles Dickens altered the ending to his novel *Great Expectations* because readers complained that it was too sad. People have altered the endings of some of Shakespeare's plays for the same reason. Is it possible to make the ending of *Of Mice and Men* a happy one? Discuss the problems in pairs. Why might it be only a temporary happy ending at best?

Changing the ending

Write a version in which Lennie and George escape. What happens to them? Alternatively invent some event that breaks up Lennie's talk with Curley's wife (thus avoiding the fatal consequences) and perhaps takes both Curley and his wife away from the farm. Compare the happy ending with the real one. Decide whether any happy ending is wrong for this book.

Missing parts of the story

1 'Well, I wasn't gonna stay no place where I couldn't get nowhere or make something of myself an' where they stole your letters. I ast her if she stole it, too, an' she says no. So I married Curley. Met him out to the Riverside Dance Palace that same night.'

Write the scene in which Curley and his wife met. What will she talk about? How might Curley seem attractive to her for a short time in her present mood?

2 'Jus' wanted to feel that little girl's dress – jus' wanted to pet it like it was a mouse – Well, how the hell did she know you jus' wanted to feel her dress?'

Write the incident in Weed. You must find a reason for George not being near Lennie at the time. Does he hear the uproar and come running? Does Lennie run and George have to find him? How did Lennie start talking to the little girl?

A report

Curley tells Whit to go and fetch Al Wilts, the deputy sheriff, from Soledad. Wilts will try to establish how Curley's wife and Lennie met their deaths. He will question the main characters.
Write the report he delivers to the sheriff. He probably won't be able to come to any definite conclusions but he will be able, by asking the right people the right questions, to establish roughly what has been happening at the ranch. This is how the report might start.

'At 2.30 on Monday, August 19th, I was called to the Toledo ranch to investigate a suspected homicide. The victim was lying in the barn on a pile of hay with her neck broken. She was . . .'

(Al Wilts will soon have a second body on his hands. Presumably Slim and George will bring Lennie's body to the ranch. Wilts will have questioned everybody concerned before making the report.)

Guess the characters

Study the photograph. How do the
expressions on the men's faces show their
feelings about Lennie? Guess which character
is which.

Further study activities

A conversation

Lennie and George will have had the same kind of conversations you read in *Of Mice and Men* many times before. Rehearse one such conversation in pairs (you can script it first if you wish) and present it to the rest of the class:

1 The conversation before they went to get their workcards.

2 The conversation when they came in sight of the farm on their first morning.

3 George goes to buy a new hat. Lennie goes with him to the shop.

The minor characters' views

1 Write what Lennie's partner on the first morning of bucking barley told his friends when he returned to the bunk-house. (Remember Slim's saying, 'He damn near killed his partner'.)

2 Write what the Boss said to his wife about Lennie and George after his first meeting with them.
(Remember how suspicious he was of George; he even thought he might be pocketing Lennie's wages.)

3 Write what Curley's wife's mother thought when she left home. (Had she really hidden the film producer's letter?)

A report

Write a newspaper report on the deaths of Curley's wife and Lennie. As a reporter, you will have spoken to Al Wilts and to people with such contrasting views as Slim and Curley. Invent a headline; include quotations from the characters.

Discussion

What would happen to people such as Lennie in today's society? What do you think should be done?
Would he be too dangerous to be free or could there be precautions taken that would make it almost impossible for him to do any really 'bad things'? You will have to decide the exact type of circumstances that will get Lennie into trouble. (Remember the girl in Weed and how Crooks had suddenly to stop his teasing of Lennie.)

A film

Imagine you have to film *Of Mice and Men* for television. Explain what locations you would look for. What instructions would you give the main actors? Which parts of the book would you concentrate on?
What problems would there be? How might you overcome them?

Speeches

Imagine George is in court on trial for the murder of Lennie. Write the opening speeches of the defence and prosecuting lawyers. Facts speak generally against George. Could it also be established that he knew just how dangerous Lennie was?
Feelings will be mostly on George's side, showing his constant care and love for Lennie.

Wider reading

At the end of most sections in this book there are suggestions for wider reading. The aim is not simply to encourage you to read more, but to read extracts or complete books that will enable you to develop a better understanding and a clearer appreciation of your set texts, by comparison and contrast of subject matter, method and style. The extracts on pages 22 to 26, for instance, will help you to understand Steinbeck and *Of Mice and Men* more clearly. If they interest you, try reading the whole of *The Grapes of Wrath* (hard but rewarding) and *Cannery Row*.

A *Kestrel for a Knave* (Section 2) also provides a useful comparison with *Of Mice and Men*; both main characters are sadly inadequate because of circumstances beyond their control. Jo is a similar victim in *A Taste of Honey* (see Section 3).

Steinbeck's people

Steinbeck's books show a concern for poor people, for outcasts, for the simple-minded and the weak-spirited. Most people are decent. Steinbeck seems to be saying, if you treat them decently. And if they're not, there's usually a good reason – Curley is an example.

The following two passages introduce you to more of Steinbeck's characters. The first is from *The Grapes of Wrath* in which Steinbeck traces the misfortunes of the farming people in Oklahoma, turned out of their land by big companies, as they seek a new life in California. Their awful journey to California ends in bitter disappointment.

The first piece is set at a cafe/gasoline station. The migrating people in broken-down transport of all kinds pour along the highway throughout the day and night. One family stops at Mae's station. Al and Bill are two lorry drivers in the cafe.

Discussion

Discuss what kind of people Mae, Al and Bill
are when you have read the passage.

A 1926 Nash sedan pulled wearily off the highway. The back seat was piled
nearly to the ceiling with sacks, with pots and pans, and on the very top, right
up against the ceiling, two boys rode. On the top of the car, a mattress and a
folded tent; tent poles tied along the running-board. The car pulled up to the
petrol pumps. A dark-haired, hatchet-faced man got slowly out. And the two
boys slid down from the load and hit the ground.

Mae walked around the counter and stood in the door. The man was
dressed in grey wool trousers and a blue shirt, dark blue with sweat on the
back and under the arms. The boys in overalls and nothing else, ragged
patched overalls. Their hair was light, and it stood up evenly all over their
heads, for it had been roached. Their faces were streaked with dust. They
went directly to the mud puddle under the hose and dug their toes into the
mud.

The man asked: 'Can we git some water, ma'am?'

A look of annoyance crossed Mae's face. 'Sure, go ahead.' She said softly
over her shoulder: 'I'll keep my eye on the hose.' She watched while the man
slowly unscrewed the radiator cap and ran the hose in.

A woman in the car, a flaxen-haired woman, said: 'See if you can't git it
here.'

The man turned off the hose and screwed on the cap again. The little boys
took the hose from him and they upended it and drank thirstily. The man took
off his dark, stained hat and stood with a curious humility in front of the
screen. 'Could you see your way to sell us a loaf of bread, ma'am?'

Mae said: 'This ain't a grocery store. We got bread to make san'widges.'

'I know, ma'am.' His humility was insistent. 'We need bread and there ain't
nothin' for quite a piece, they say.'

''F we sell bread we gonna run out.' Mae's tone was faltering.

'We're hungry,' the man said.

'Whyn't you buy a san'widge? We got nice san'widges, hamburgs.'

'We'd sure admire to do that, ma'am. But we can't. We got to make a dime
do all of us.' And he said embarrassedly: 'We ain't got but a little.'

Mae said: 'You can't get no loaf a bread for a dime. We only got fifteen-
cent loafs.'

From behind her Al growled: 'God Almighty, Mae, give 'em bread.'

'We'll run out 'fore the bread truck comes.'

'Run out, then, goddamn it,' said Al. And he looked sullenly down at the
potato salad he was mixing.

Mae shrugged her plump shoulders and looked to the truck drivers to show
them what she was up against.

She held the screen door open and the man came in, bringing a smell of
sweat with him. The boys edged in behind him and they went immediately to

the candy case and stared in – not with craving or with hope or even with desire, but just with a kind of wonder that such things could be. They were alike in size and their faces were alike. One scratched his dusty ankle with the toe-nails of his other foot. The other whispered some soft message and then they straightened their arms so that their clenched fists in the overall pockets showed through the thin blue cloth.

Mae opened the drawer and took out a long waxpaper-wrapped loaf. 'This here is a fifteen-cent loaf.'

The man put his hat back on his head. He answered with inflexible humility: 'Won't you – can't you see your way to cut off ten cents' worth?'

Al said snarlingly: 'Goddamn it, Mae. Give 'em the loaf.'

The man turned toward Al. 'No, we want to buy ten cents' worth of it. We got it figgered awful close, mister, to get to California.'

Mae said resignedly: 'You can have this for ten cents.'

'That'd be robbin' you, ma'am.'

'Go ahead – Al says to take it.' She pushed the waxpapered loaf across the counter. The man took a deep leather pouch from his rear pocket, untied the strings, and spread it open. It was heavy with silver and with greasy bills.

'May soun' funny to be so tight,' he apologized. 'We got a thousan' miles to go, an' we don' know if we'll make it.' He dug in the pouch with a forefinger, located a dime, and pinched in for it. When he put it down on the counter he had a penny with it. He was about to drop the penny back into the pouch when his eye fell on the boys frozen before the candy counter. He moved slowly down to them. He pointed in the case at big long sticks of striped peppermint. 'Is them penny candy, ma'am?'

Mae moved down and looked in. 'Which ones?'

'There, them stripy ones.'

The little boys raised their eyes to her face and they stopped breathing; their mouths were partly opened, their half-naked bodies were rigid.

'Oh – them. Well, no – them's two for a penny.'

'Well, gimme two then, ma'am.' He placed the copper cent carefully on the counter. The boys expelled their held breath softly. Mae held the big sticks out.

'Take 'em,' said the man.

They reached timidly, each took a stick, and they held them down at their sides and did not look at them. But they looked at each other, and their mouth corners smiled rigidly with embarrassment.

'Thank you, ma'am.' The man picked up the bread and went out the door, and the little boys marched stiffly behind him, the red-striped sticks held tightly against their legs. They leaped like chipmunks over the front seat and on to the top of the load, and they burrowed back out of sight like chipmunks.

The man got in and started his car, and with a roaring motor and a cloud of blue oily smoke the ancient Nash climbed up on the highway and went on its way to the west.

From inside the restaurant the truck drivers and Mae and Al stared after them.

Big Bill wheeled back. 'Them wasn't two-for-a-cent candy,' he said.

'What's that to you?' Mae said fiercely.

'Them was nickel apiece candy,' said Bill.

'We got to get goin',' said the other man. 'We're droppin' time.' They reached in their pockets. Bill put a coin on the counter and the other man looked at it and reached again and put down a coin. They swung around and walked to the door.

'So long,' said Bill.

Mae called: 'Hey! Wait a minute. You got change.'

'You go to hell,' said Bill, and the screen door slammed.

Mae watched them get into the great truck, watched it lumber off in low gear and heard the shift up the whining gears to cruising ratio. 'Al-' she said softly.

He looked up from the hamburger he was patting thin and stacking between waxed papers. 'What ya want?'

'Look there.' She pointed at the coins beside the cups – two half-dollars. Al walked near and looked, and then he went back to his work.

'Truck drivers,' Mae said reverently, 'an' after them shit-heels.'

from Grapes of Wrath by John Steinbeck

In the second passage, the people of the ramshackle Cannery Row are going to throw a secret party for Doc – in his own house – for the favours and help he has given them. Doc hears about the secret party and carefully packs all his valuable specimens out of harm's way – he knows from experience the mayhem that is likely to result from his 'friends' drinking too much. Still, they mean well and everybody is looking for a present for Doc, including Frankie, whom Doc has looked after for many years.

Discussion

1 Decide in what way Frankie is similar to Lennie. How does Doc try to cover his emotions?

2 Do you find this and the previous passage moving in the same way as parts of *Of Mice and Men*?

3 How is Steinbeck able to make the reader share his characters' feelings?

Sooner or later Frankie was bound to hear about the party. For Frankie drifted about like a small cloud. He was always on the edge of groups. No one noticed him or paid any attention to him. You couldn't tell whether he was listening of not. But Frankie did hear about the party and he heard about the presents and a feeling of fullness swelled in him and a feeling of sick longing.

In the window of Jacob's Jewellery Store was the most beautiful thing in the world. It had been there a long time. It was a black onyx clock with a gold face, but on top of it was the real beauty. On top was a bronze group – St. George killing the dragon. The dragon was on his back with his claws in the air and in his breast was St. George's spear. The Saint was in full armour, with the visor raised, and he rode a fat, big-buttocked horse. With his spear he pinned the dragon to the ground. But the wonderful thing was that he wore a pointed beard and he looked a little like Doc.

Frankie walked to Alvarado Street several times a week to stand in front of the window and look at this beauty. He dreamed about it too, dreamed of running his fingers over the rich, smooth bronze. He had known about it for months when he heard of the party and the presents.

Frankie stood on the pavement for an hour before he went inside. 'Well?' said Mr. Jacobs. He had given Frankie a visual searching as he came in and he knew there wasn't seventy-five cents on him.

'How much is that?' Frankie asked huskily.

'What?'

'That.'

'You mean the clock? Fifty dollars – with the group seventy-five dollars.'

Frankie walked out without replying. He went down to the beach and crawled under an overturned rowboat and peeked out at the little waves. The bronze beauty was so strong in his head that it seemed to stand out in front of him. And a frantic trapped feeling came over him. He had to get the beauty. His eyes were fierce when he thought of it.

He stayed under the boat all day and at night he emerged and went back to Alvarado Street. While people went to the movies and came out and went to the Golden Poppy, he walked up and down the block. And he didn't get tired or sleepy, for the beauty burned in him like fire.

At last the people thinned out and gradually disappeared from the streets and the parked cars drove away and the town settled to sleep.

A policeman looked closely at Frankie. 'What you doing out?' he asked.

Frankie took to his heels and fled around the corner and hid behind a barrel in the alley. At two-thirty he crept to the door of Jacob's and tried the knob. It was locked. Frankie went back to the alley and sat behind the barrel and thought. He saw a broken piece of concrete lying beside the barrel and he picked it up.

The policeman reported that he heard the crash and ran to it. Jacob's window was broken. He saw the prisoner walking rapidly away and chased him. He didn't know how the boy could run that far and that fast carrying fifty pounds of clock and bronze, but the prisoner nearly got away. If he had not blundered into a blind street he would have got away.

The chief called Doc the next day. 'Come on down, will you? I want to talk to you.'

They brought Frankie in very dirty and frowzy. His eyes were red, but he held his mouth firm and he even smiled a little welcome when he saw Doc.

'What's the matter, Frankie?' Doc asked.

'He broke into Jacob's last night,' the chief said. 'Stole some stuff. We got in touch with his mother. She says it's not her fault, because he hangs around your place all the time.'

'Frankie – you shouldn't have done it,' said Doc. The heavy stone of inevitability was on his heart. 'Can't you parole him to me?' Doc asked.

'I don't think the judge will do it,' said the chief. 'We've got a mental report. You know what's wrong with him?'

'Yes,' said Doc. 'I know.'

'And you know what's likely to happen when he comes into puberty?'

'Yes,' said Doc, 'I know,' and the stone weighed terribly on his heart.

'The doctor thinks we better put him away. We couldn't before, but now he's got a felony on him, I think we better.'

As Frankie listened the welcome died in his eyes.

'What did he take?' Doc asked.

'A great big clock and a bronze statue.'

'I'll pay for it.'

'Oh, we got it back. I don't think the judge will hear of it. It'll just happen again. You know that.'

'Yes,' said Doc softly, 'I know. But maybe he had a reason. Frankie,' he said, 'why did you take it?'

Frankie looked a long time at him. 'I love you,' he said.

Doc ran out and got in his car and went collecting in the caves below Pt. Lobes.

from *Cannery Row* by John Steinbeck

2

A Kestrel for a Knave

Barry Hines

One day in the life of Billy Casper

Kes or *A Kestrel for a Knave* is about one day in the life of Billy Casper. He is fifteen years old and just about to leave school. We follow him through his day from waking up to going to bed. He does an early-morning paper round, goes to school where he gets into trouble as usual, first at registration and then for sleeping in assembly, for which he gets caned. We see him doing an English lesson, fighting and losing in the playground, forced to play a game of football, feeding and training his kestrel and finally coming home to find that the hawk has been killed by his brother, Jud. The killing is an act of revenge. Billy has used Jud's betting money, left with him by Jud to put on a racing double, to buy food for himself and his hawk. In a series of flashbacks, during Billy's day, we learn how he came to catch and tame the hawk.

Billy is a little like the animal he has tamed. Billy, too, lives in a savage world. For Billy, it is full of enemies. Sometimes he can outwit them but he can never defeat them. His mother is selfish and gives no thought to Billy's welfare. Jud, his half-brother, is like her but far more brutal. Some of Billy's enemies, however, such as his form master, Mr Crossley, his headmaster, Mr Gryce, and Sugden, the PE teacher, do not act out of pure selfishness or an evil wish to torment Billy. They see him as an outsider whom they must try to fit into their respectable world. Billy, poor, physically weak, often cold and hungry, has no way of getting into that world, even if he wanted to. He can not really see how it works. His understanding of why things happen to him is not very clear. Rather like a wild animal he lives mainly in the present, not giving much thought to the future or the past.

Billy, however, like his hawk, has some resources. Billy's feelings for nature and his strength of character bring some light into his dark world. He has the courage to capture the kestrel and the endless patience needed to tame it. Because of the hawk Billy comes to know success and self-respect and a vision of wildness and space far beyond the narrow bleakness of the town where he lives. Because of that it is all the more tragic for Billy when the hawk is killed.

Detailed study of the text

The text has been divided up under seven headings. Page numbers refer to the Penguin edition of *Kes*. The relevant study projects are given under each heading. More general questions on the whole book follow this section.

Early morning paper round
(pages 7–21)

Discussion

Petty crimes such as Billy commits, stealing from Mr Porter and the milkman, could be punished by a fine or probation or both. Do you think Billy would deserve such punishment or is there something to be said in his defence?

Doing the job

Billy has a lot of papers to deliver very quickly on a cold morning. In what ways could his home have better equipped him to do the job? Write a list or a short paragraph about it.

Mr Porter

Does Mr Porter know about Billy's home? Does he like Billy or does he employ him because he can get no one else? Does he know that Billy steals things from him but allows it? Write, as if you were Mr Porter, a short conversation you have with a customer about Billy.

Clues

We know later that Billy is interested in wild things. Which short passage in this section, when Billy is delivering the papers, shows you that Billy does have an interest in nature?

Film or video

You are the designer for a film or video to be made of the book. Your producer has asked you to pick the scenes for this section, keeping to as few scenes as possible. In a sentence or two say what you think these opening scenes should be and give a few words of description of each.

Illustration

Either draw or describe the Caspers' living room (on this particular morning) as an illustration to this section, *or* choose something yourself which you think would be a better illustration for this section and draw or describe that.

The taking of the hawk
(pages 21–44)

Twosomes

Either in group discussion or in writing, identify each of the two people talking together below and say where they are at the time.

1 'No, 'cos I'm not goin' to work down t'pit.'
   'Where are tha' goin' to work, then ?'

2 'There's no nest up there, so off you go.'
   'There is. I've seen it fly in.'

3 'I don't want to wait that long. I want a book today.'
   'You'll just have to want, won't you?'

4 'I've cleaned t'bottom shed out ready, an' I've built a little nesting box out of an orange box 'til . . .'
   'Ten to eight! Ee, I'm goin' to be late as usual.'

Writing

Apart from taking the young hawk from its nest, what other things does Billy do in this section which show us how interested he is in nature and the wild?

School I (morning): assembly, a caning, an English lesson
(pages 45–85)

Discussion

1 Discuss the ways in which Billy's school is like and unlike the one you attend. Compare the two schools, deciding which is better in terms of learning conditions, discipline, activities and so on.

2 Have you ever been told off or punished at school like Billy, without really knowing why? Explain what happened and how you felt.

Group activity

In groups discuss what some of Billy's teachers might think of him. Consider what might be the attitude of Mr Crossley, Mr Gryce or Mr Farthing towards him. You might invent one or two other teachers, sympathetic or not sympathetic to Billy. Then act out, in character, the discussion – or argument – the teachers might have about Billy in the Staff Room.

Writing

1 Write Billy's school report, including short reports from his teachers and from Mr Gryce, the headmaster.

2 The small boy on the bicycle goes home and tells his mother about meeting Billy with his hawk. Write their conversation in the form of a play or as speech.

Film or video

In a film or video the actors are picked to look like the characters depicted in the book. Draw, or describe in words, the following people as you think they should appear on film or tape: Mr Crossley, MacDowall, Anderson, Mr Gryce, Mr Farthing. Add to each drawing or description a sentence or two giving the approximate age you think they are, something of their physical appearance – tall or short, fat or thin, well-dressed or shabby – whether they are, if adult, married or unmarried, what sort of home they live in and what their hobbies or interests might be.

Notes for the reader

Billy uses a lot of technical falconer's words such as 'creance', 'lure' and 'bating'. List all the technical words you can find in his conversation with Mr Farthing in front of the class (pages 64 to 69 in the Penguin edition) and, using your copy of *Kes* or a dictionary, explain what each term means.

School II (morning): the football match (pages 85–108)

Discussion

1 Should some kinds of sport be compulsory in schools? If so, what kinds of sport? Or should all kinds of sport be optional and take place after school? Does competitive sport build character or does great emphasis on who wins or loses create problems? What effect did competitive sport have on Billy?

2 Because he is bored, Billy plays with the goal net, pretending to be a lion. What sort of things do you find yourself doing when you are bored or what sort of things have you noticed other people doing when they are bored?

Role play

'He's had enough, Sir.'

Some of the boys with Billy might be on his side but be afraid to say so because of Sugden. Some might enjoy tormenting Billy. Some might be against Billy because of his attitude. Pick those characters who might be for or against Billy. You can take names from the book like Purdey or Ellis or Tibbut or Anderson and argue about Billy's behaviour in the match and Sugden's treatment of him. Was this treatment fair? You might go on to argue about Billy's behaviour generally, his family life, his stealing, his life in school.

Writing

1 Sugden talks that evening to a friend about the 'match'. Describe, as if you were Sugden, what went on and how well you did.

2 Write part of the news commentary on the match in which Billy played.

3 Write a news commentary about part of a match in which you have played. You could make it a fair commentary or you could write it as if you were a person like Mr Sugden.

Feeding and flying the kestrel
(pages 108–126)

Discussion

Is Billy's killing of the sparrow any worse than cattle being killed for meat? Is the description of how the hawk eats the sparrow rather sickening? Would the book be better with these two descriptions left out, or are they necessary for the story? Do they tell us something new about Billy or the hawk?

Diagrams

Use the information given in this section – or by doing some of your own research as well – to draw and label a diagram of how a lure is prepared. Then draw and label a diagram of trainer, hawk and lure, showing how the lure is used.

Writing

Using what each of them says in this section, describe how Mr Farthing feels about hawks and how Billy feels about them.

School (afternoon): career prospects (pages 126–140)

A map

Draw a sketch map of Billy's school showing the route by which Billy escapes from Jud and labelling each stage of the escape in a short phrase. You can label also the Headmaster's study, the Secretary's office, the position of the playing fields and so on.

A form to fill in

Look at the form on page 32. Do not fill in the form in this book. Write in your own book the details that would go on the form, if you were completing it for Billy. Billy's address is: 124 Woods Avenue, Bransley (this address can also be found on page 85 of the Penguin edition). You can call the town where Billy lives 'Bransley'. His school might be Bransley Boys' Secondary Modern. If there is nothing to put on the form write 'none' or 'not applicable'.

Now, bearing in mind what you know of Billy, suggest a job he might do and say why you think that could be suitable for him.

```
┌─────────────────────────────────────────────────────────────────────┐
│              BRANSLEY BOYS' SECONDARY MODERN SCHOOL                    │
│                     REFERENCE ASSESSMENT                              │
├──────────────────────┬──────────────────────┬────────────────────────┤
│ SURNAME..............│ FORM.................│ CAREER INTERESTS:      │
│ FORENAME(S).........│ DATE OF BIRTH........│                        │
│ ....................│ ....................│                        │
│ ADDRESS.............│ DATE OF ENTERING     │                        │
│ ....................│ THIS SCHOOL..........│                        │
│ ....................│ ....................│                        │
│ TEL NO:.............│                      │                        │
├──────────────────────┼──────────────────────┼────────────────────────┤
│ IN SCHOOL            │ OUT·OF SCHOOL        │ EMPLOYMENT             │
│ ACTIVITIES           │ HOBBIES              │ SATURDAYS:             │
│ INTERESTS            │ CLUBS                │                        │
│ A                    │                      │                        │
│ B                    │                      │ EVENINGS:              │
│ C                    │                      │                        │
│ D                    │                      │                        │
│ E                    │                      │                        │
└──────────────────────┴──────────────────────┴────────────────────────┘
```

Writing

1 During Billy's maths lesson and while he is running away from Jud, we get a picture of what it is like during afternoon school. Write your own description of what is going on in your school during an afternoon session.

2 Jud meets someone else beside Tibbutt and describes in detail what Billy has done, why he is looking for him and what he will do when he finds Billy. Write, in play form, the conversation that takes place. You need not try to imitate Jud's dialect speech.

Jud's revenge (pages 140–159)

Illustration

Pick one of the striking moments in this section, suitable for an illustration. Then draw it or describe what you would put in the picture.

Role play

'Ee, what a family that is.'

The neighbours would know a lot about the Caspers, the fact that the father had left home, Mrs Casper's many different men, Jud's drunkenness, Billy's stealing. Some neighbours might disapprove strongly of Billy's keeping tame animals and his hawk. Some neighbours, however, might be sympathetic, at least towards Billy. In groups of about five or six, discuss the different attitudes you might take up as the Caspers' neighbours and then act out the conversation these neighbours might have about the problem family.

Writing

1 Have you ever lost something that you missed a great deal and for which you spent a long time searching without success? Write about it, saying how long you spent looking for it and where, and how you felt at the time.

2 Does Billy's father think about the family he has left? Does he hate his wife? Does he ever think about Billy or Jud? Does he ever think about going back? Write, as if you were Billy's father, a letter to a friend or relative of his, saying how you feel about the family you have left and what plans you have.

3 If you were asked to continue the story, what would happen to Jud in your version? Write an account of Jud's future as it would happen in your book.

4 Continue Billy's story. Does he have to go down the mine? Does he grow to be more like Jud? Or do you see some hope for him? Does he find another hawk or wild animal to tame? Does he find someone to help him such as Mr Farthing? Does he even manage to get a job involving animals? Write a short account of what you think could happen to him in his four or five months after leaving school.

Billy's violent world

Use the five pictures here and on page 36 to write a piece about the violent world of Billy Casper.

Decide the incident each picture represents. Say in each case how effectively the actors have captured the feelings of their characters and how far you think Billy is the innocent victim.

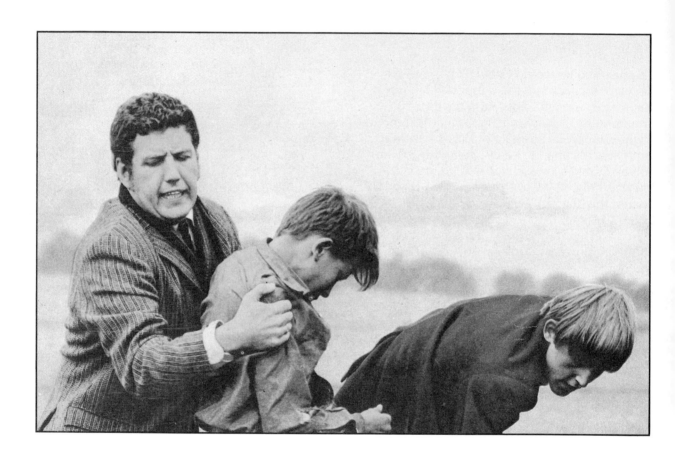

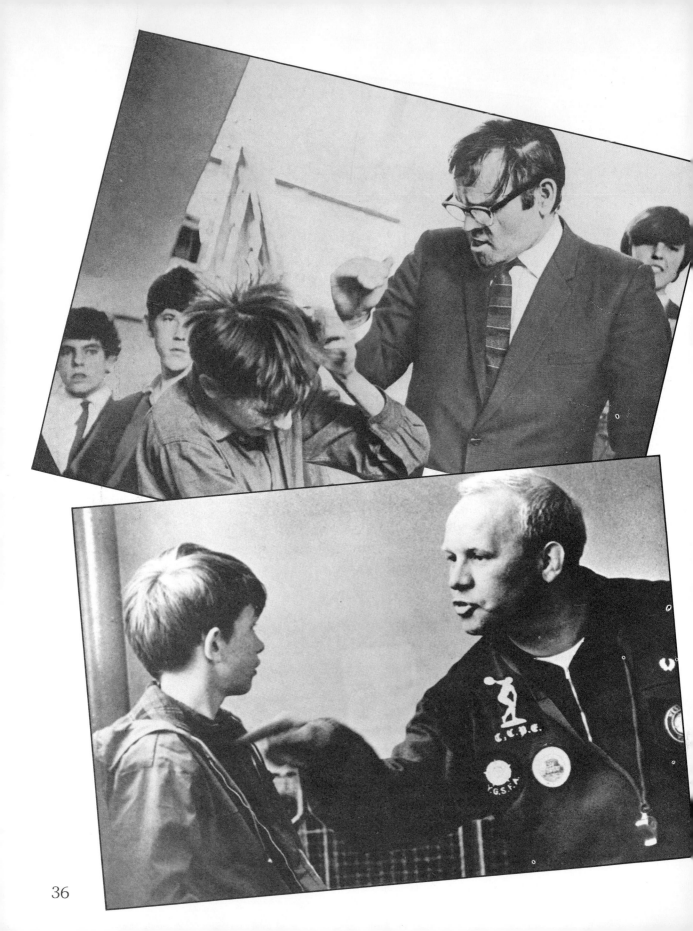

Further study activities

A plan

Draw a step plan for Billy's day. Move downwards for Billy's misfortunes and up for the pleasant things that happen. Label each step and construct your plan like this:

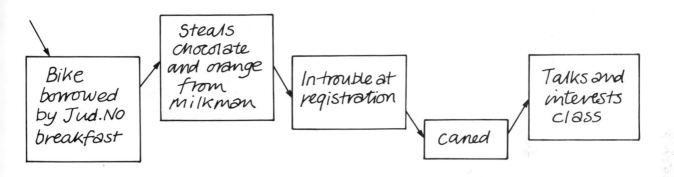

Quotations

Who says this and who is being spoken to?
1 'And so you thought you'd enlighten me and the class with your idiotic information?'

2 '. . . No guts . . . No backbone . . . you've nothing to commend you whatsoever. You're just fodder for the mass media.'

3 'You'd say I was a bully, wouldn't you, lad? And you'd be right because I'm bigger and stronger, and I know that I could beat you to a pulp before I started.'

4 'Every lesson for four years! And in all that time you've made no attempt whatsoever to get any kit, you've skyved and scrounged and borrowed and . . .'

A defence of Billy

Mr Crossley has called Billy 'idiotic', Mr Gryce has said that people like Billy have no 'guts', even Mr Farthing has called Billy a bad lad. We know that Billy is a thief. Write a defence of Billy, describing things he does and says in the book, which show that some of these judgements are wrong or that there may be reasons for Billy's bad actions.

Discussion

In the film the small boy getting caned was made amusing and Mr Sugden was a comic character. Is there humour in the book or is it all gloomy? You will justify your point of view in the discussion if you can describe incidents which you found amusing or which, though seemingly intended to be amusing, you did not find funny.

Writing

1 Who, apart from Billy, have you found the most pleasant character in the book? Write an account of that person describing what is said and done to make him or her appeal to you.

2 If Billy is the hero of *Kes*, who is the villain? Is there more than one 'villain'? Write about the villain or villains, describing what they say and do which has led you to your judgement of them.

3 Who are Mr Rogers and MacDowall? What part do they play in Billy's story?

4 Describe some of the passages in the book which showed Billy's liking for nature and those which showed that Billy found the town dreary.

Cover illustration

Pick some incident which you found very interesting or very important to the course of the story. Use that as a basis for your cover illustration and draw or describe in words the picture you would create. You might consider which of the two titles of the book you would feature, the size of print of the title and the size of print of the author's name on the cover.

Wider reading

Of Mice and Men (see Section 1) will provide you with many useful points of comparison with *A Kestrel for a Knave*. Both Lennie and Billy are victims of circumstances beyond their control. Lennie's end is tragic, Billy's almost as sad – he goes back to his awful house because there is no alternative. You could compare the authors' and other characters' attitudes to Billy and Lennie.

To what extent do characters such as Lennie and Billy bring out the worst and best in human nature?

One important difference between Lennie and Billy is that Lennie's tragedy springs from his mental disorder while Billy's is caused by his social deprivation – there is nothing wrong with Billy that a different home and school environment wouldn't cure.

If you wished to look at other novels about the effects of a hostile environment you could try:

Down and Out in Paris and London – George Orwell;
The History of Mr Polly – H. G. Wells;
Lord of the Flies – William Golding.

GCSE Examination Boards are particularly keen that some of your wider reading goes beyond contemporary authors. *Mr Polly* (written 1910) is a funny/sad book in which the main character is trapped through no fault of his own in an environment for which he is not suited.

Z for Zachariah (Section 10) shows a hostile environment at its most extreme.

Jo in *A Taste of Honey* also lives in a hostile environment (Section 3) and can be usefully compared with Billy in *A Kestrel for a Knave*.

Short stories: As a contrast to reading about children being mistreated by adults, read 'The Lumber Room' and 'The Destructors', both in *Twentieth Century Short Stories* (Harrap). In both stories the roles are reversed and the children conquer, though Trevor, in 'The Destructor's is hardly a person you will like to identify with.

3

A Taste of Honey

Shelagh Delaney

Looking at stage directions

One striking feature of *A Taste of Honey* is the absence of stage directions, particularly at the beginning. Look at the directions at the beginning of *An Inspector Calls*. You are told the type of room, the furniture, the positions of the actors, their ages, appearances and even their present mood:

The dining-room of a fairly large suburban house, belonging to a prosperous manufacturer. It has good solid furniture of the period. The general effect is substantial and heavily comfortable, but not cosy and homelike. (If a realistic set is used, then it should be swung back, as it was in the production at the New Theatre. By doing this, you can have the dining-table centre downstage during Act One, when it is needed there, and then, swinging back, can reveal the fireplace for Act Two, and then for Act Three can show a small table with telephone on it, downstage of fireplace; and by this time the dining-table and its chairs have moved well upstage. Producers who wish to avoid this tricky business, which involves two resettings of the scene and some very accurate adjustments of the extra flats necessary, would be well advised to dispense with an ordinary realistic set, if only because the dining-table becomes a nuisance. The lighting should be pink and intimate until the Inspector arrives, and then it should be brighter and harder.)

At rise of curtain, the four Birlings and Gerald are seated at the table, with Arthur Birling at one end, his wife at the other, Eric downstage, and Sheila and Gerald seated upstage. Edna, the parlourmaid, is just clearing the table, which has no cloth, of dessert plates and champagne glasses, etc., and then replacing them with decanter of port, cigar box and cigarettes. Port glasses are already on the table. All five are in evening dress of the period, the men in tails and white ties, not dinner-jackets. Arthur Birling is a heavy-looking, rather portentous man in his middle fifties with fairly easy manners but rather provincial in his speech. His wife is about fifty, a rather cold woman and her husband's social superior. Sheila is a pretty girl in her early twenties, very pleased with life and rather excited. Gerald Croft is an attractive chap about thirty, rather too manly to be a dandy but very much the easy well-bred young man-about-town. Eric is in his early twenties, not quite at ease, half shy, half assertive. At the moment they have all had a good dinner, are celebrating a special occasion, and are pleased with themselves.

In contrast, *A Taste of Honey* opens with:

The stage represents a comfortless flat in Manchester and the street outside. Jazz music. Enter Helen, a semi-whore and her daughter, Jo. They are loaded with baggage.

Sheila Delaney, the author, has left more decision-making to the director than J. B. Priestley who wrote *An Inspector Calls*. Nevertheless, she gives us more details about the room's appearance through the dialogue.

Write detailed stage directions

Imagine you wished to give more guidance to the director of *A Taste of Honey*. Write detailed directions, similar to those in *An Inspector Calls*. You will need to make your own interpretation of what Jo and Helen are wearing, their appearances and their moods. You will find details of the room by looking through the dialogue in Act One, but you can add some of your own ideas. What, for instance, is in the baggage they are loaded with? Like their clothes and general appearances, it will have to fit in with your idea of the right atmosphere for the start of the play.

A critic's view

Read this comment by a reviewer:

> I doubt very much whether Miss Delaney had any particular theme in mind, anything she wanted to say, when she sat down to write *A Taste of Honey*. She probably came too young (aged 19) to her composition to have any theories to expound.
>
> 'Here are some people that I know about,' she said in effect to her audience, 'and here is what happened to them.' And because she really did know about them, and really understood them, her play still holds its place in the theatre.
>
> I find the play unsatisfactory because I have a prejudice in favour of the dramatist who has something to say, and who invents characters to say it. The characters, while coming alive in their own right, interact in such a way that the author's theme is illustrated.
>
> But in *A Taste of Honey* the characters hardly interact at all. They slip in and out of each other's lives, but hardly influence each other at all, although each comes vividly to life in him or herself.
>
> W. H. Darlington, *London Theatre Record*

There are so many points about the play in this comment that it can be used to form the basis of a study of the play.

'Some people that I know'

There are five characters in the play. What kind of people are they?
Below are two quotations said by others about each character. Decide for
each character how far these quotations sum them up. What is left out? Add
quotations both to confirm the view already given and to show other sides of
their characters.

Helen

Jo   She had so much love for everyone else, but none for me.

Geof   She always said you were a pretty rotten sort of woman.
       I thought she was exaggerating.

Are these comments fair to Helen? What can be said in her defence?

Jo

Helen   . . . I would never have dared to have talked to my mother like that
        when I was her age . . .

Helen   You had to throw yourself at the first man you met, didn't you.

Is Jo really promiscuous? How independent is she? How good a mother will
she be?

Peter

Jo   I bet you've had thousands of girl friends.

Helen   He threw his money about like a man with no arms.

Peter is a brash car salesman, cigar in mouth. Is Peter just a stock drunk in a
play, or is there more to him than that? Why might Helen attract him?

Geof

Helen   How long is he going to stay here? Bloody little pansy.

Jo   You know, I've got so used to old Geof lying there on that couch –
     like an old watchdog.

What makes Geof possibly the most interesting character in the play? In what
ways is he kind and tender? How does he differ from the stock homosexual
mocked by comedians?

Boy

Jo   I know you're only after one thing.

Jo   He could sing and dance and he was as black as coal.

The boy leaves Jo pregnant. Is there anything that can be said in his
defence?

The characters' relationships

The critic said the characters drifted in and out of each other's lives, but that they didn't affect each other. To find out if you agree or not, it is important to look for evidence in the play.

Four short extracts follow. They are among the first words the particular pairs of characters say to each other during the play. Study the relationships between each pair by acting out each piece. Take it in turn to perform. Work in small groups, the non-performers helping to direct by suggesting different ways the lines could be said.

Extract one

Helen   Well! This is the place.

Jo   And I don't like it.

Helen   When I find somewhere for us to live I have to consider something far more important than your feelings . . . the rent. It's all I can afford.

Jo   You can afford something better than this old ruin.

Helen   When you start earning you can start moaning.

Jo   Can't be soon enough for me. I'm cold and my shoes let water . . . what a place . . . and we're supposed to be living off her immoral earnings.

Helen   I'm careful. Anyway, what's wrong with this place? Everything in it's falling apart, it's true, and we've no heating — but there's a lovely view of the gasworks, we share a bathroom with the community and this wallpaper's contemporary. What more do you want? Anyway it'll do for us. Pass me a glass, Jo.

Jo   Where are they?

Helen   I don't know.

Jo   You packed 'em. She'd lose her head if it was loose.

Helen   Here they are. I put 'em in my bag for safety. Pass me that bottle — it's in the carrier.

Jo   Why should I run round after you? [*Takes whisky bottle from bag.*]

Helen   Children owe their parents these little attentions.

Jo   I don't owe you a thing.

Helen   Except respect, and I don't seem to get any of that.

What sort of relationship is there between mother and daughter? Is it more like two quarrelling sisters? Are they really angry with each other, or are they so used to a kind of joking relationship that there are no strong feelings underneath the words?

Try to act the piece both ways: really angry and then casually joking.

Discussion

Has the relationship between Jo and Helen changed at the end of the play? Look at the conversation between them at the end.

Extract two

Helen   Oh! Throw that cigar away. It looks bloody horrible stuck in your mouth like a horizontal chimney.

Peter   Your nose is damp. Here, have this.

Helen   Oh go away!

Peter   Give it a good blow.

Helen   Leave it alone.

Peter   Blow your nose, woman. [*She does*]. And while you're at it blow a few of those cobwebs out of your head. You can't afford to lose a man like me.

Helen   Can't I?

Peter   This is the old firm. You can't renege on the old firm.

Helen   I'm a free lance. Besides, I'm thinking of giving it up.

Peter   What?

Helen   Sex! Men!

Peter   What have we done to deserve this?

Helen   It's not what you've done. It's what I've done.

Peter   But [*approaching her*], darling, you do it so well.

Helen   Now give over, Peter. I've got all these things to unpack.

Peter   Send her to the pictures.

Helen   I don't feel like it.

Peter   What's wrong?

Helen   I'm tired. It's terrible when you've got a cold, isn't it? You don't fancy anything.

Peter   Well, put your hat on, let's go for a drink. Come on down to the church and I'll make an honest woman of you.

Helen   [*she goes to put her coat on, then changes her mind*]: No, I don't fancy it.

Peter   I'm offering to marry you, dear.

Helen	You what?
Peter	Come on, let's go for a drink.
Helen	I told you I don't fancy it.
Peter	You won't find anything better.
Helen	Listen, love, I'm old enough to be your mother.
Peter	[*petting her*]: Now you know I like this mother and son relationship.
Helen	Stop it!
Peter	Aren't you wearing your girdle?
Helen	Now, Peter.
Peter	Whoops!

What feelings have Helen and Peter for each other? Is he joking or serious in lines such as: 'What have we done to deserve this?' and 'I'm offering to marry you, dear'?
Does she mean what she is saying in lines such as: 'I don't fancy it' and 'Stop it!'?
In acting out the lines try casual, joking and serious methods.

Discussion

Do Helen's and Peter's feelings for each other
stay the same throughout the play?

Extract three

Boy   You mean it too. You're the first girl I've met who really didn't care. Listen, I'm going to ask you something. I'm a man of few words. Will you marry me?

Jo   Well, I'm a girl of few words. I won't marry you but you've talked me into it.

Boy   How old are you?

Jo   Nearly eighteen.

Boy   And you really will marry me?

Jo   I said so, didn't I? You shouldn't have asked me if you were only kidding me up. [*She starts to go.*]

Boy   Hey! I wasn't kidding. I thought you were. Do you really mean it? You will marry me?

Jo   I love you.

Boy   How do you know?

Jo   I don't know why I love you but I do.

Boy   I adore you. [*Swinging her through the air.*]

Jo   So do I. I can't resist myself.

Boy   I've got something for you.

Jo   What is it? A ring!

Boy   This morning in the shop I couldn't remember what sort of hands you had, long hands, small hands or what. I stood there like a damn fool trying to remember what they felt like. [*He puts the ring on and kisses her hand.*] What will your mother say?

Jo   She'll probably laugh.

Boy   Doesn't she care who her daughter marries?

Jo   She's not marrying you, I am. It's got nothing to do with her.

The line 'Hey! I wasn't kidding. I thought you were.' provides a clue as to how to play the scene. Jo is in love but is afraid; she means the 'I love you', but always counters an honest expression of her feelings with a joke.
Try out Jo's uncertainty in your acting of the passage.

Extract four

Geof   I'll put the light on.

Jo   No, you won't! I like this romantic half-light, it just goes with this Manchester maisonette!

Geof   Take four paces forward, turn right, turn left, once round the gasworks and straight on up the creek. [*He bangs into a chair or table and cries or swears.*]

Jo   Put a match on, you daft thing.
[*Geof strikes a match.*]

Geof   Ee, this place is enormous, isn't it?

Jo   I know. I've got to work all day in a shoe shop and all night in a bar to pay for it. But it's mine. All mine.

Geof   I can tell it's yours from the state it's in. No wonder you won't put the light on. Where do you keep the cups?

Jo   In the sink.

Geof   Isn't this place a bit big for one, Jo?

Jo   Why? Are you thinking of moving in?

Geof   Not likely.

Jo   You are, you know. Put 'em down here. Don't you want any?

Geof   No.

Jo   Well, hand 'em over to me because I'm starved. Has your landlady thrown you out?

Geof   Don't be silly.

Jo   I've been wondering why you were so anxious to see me home. You didn't fancy sleeping under the arches, did you? Why did your landlady throw you out, Geoffrey? I'll let you stay here if you tell me.

Geof   I was behind with the rent.

Jo   That's a lie for a start.

Geof   I don't tell lies.

Jo   Come on, let's have some truth. Why did she throw you out?

Geof   I've told you why.

Jo   [*switches on light*]: Come on, the truth. Who did she find you with? Your girl friend? It wasn't a man, was it?

Geof   Don't be daft.

Jo   Look, I've got a nice comfortable couch, I've even got some sheets. You can stay here if you'll tell me what you do. Go on, I've always wanted to know about people like you.

Geof   Go to hell.

Jo   I won't snigger, honest I won't. Tell me some of it, go on. I bet you never told a woman before.

Geof   I don't go in for sensational confessions.

Jo   I want to know what you do. I want to know why you do it. Tell me or get out.

Geof   Right! [*He goes to the door.*]

Jo	Geof, don't go. Don't go. Geof! I'm sorry. Please stay.
Geof	Don't touch me.
Jo	I didn't mean to hurt your feelings.
Geof	I can't stand women at times. Let go of me.
Jo	Come on, Geof. I don't care what you do.
Geof	Thank you. May I go now, please?
Jo	Please stay here Geof. I'll get those sheets and blankets.
Geof	I can't stand people who laugh at other people. They'd get a bigger laugh if they laughed at themselves.
Jo	Please stay, Geof. [*She goes off for the sheets and blankets. He finds her book of drawings on the table and glances through them.*]
Geof	Are these yours?
Jo	No, why? Put them down, Geof.
Geof	Obviously they are. They're exactly like you.
Jo	How do you mean?
Geof	Well, there's no design, rhythm or purpose.
Jo	Hey?
Geof	Where's the design in that? It's all messy, isn't it? Charcoal. I don't like it.
Jo	I do.
Geof	What made you choose that for a subject?
Jo	I like . . .
Geof	They're all sentimental!
Jo	Me? Sentimental?
Geof	No. No. I don't like 'em.
Jo	Do you really think they're sentimental?
Geof	Well, look. I mean . . .
Jo	I'm sorry you don't like them.
Geof	Why don't you go to a decent school?
Jo	I've never been to any school.
Geof	You want taking in hand.
Jo	No, thanks.
Geof	Has anybody ever tried?
Jo	What?
Geof	Taking you in hand.
Jo	Yes.
Geof	What happened to him?
Jo	He came in with Christmas and went out with the New Year.
Geof	Did you like him?
Jo	He was all right . . .
Geof	Did you love him?
Jo	I don't know much about love. I've never been too familiar with it. I suppose I must have loved him. They say love creates. And I'm certainly creating at the moment. I'm going to have a baby.

from *A Taste of Honey* by Shelagh Delaney

What does the passage tell you about the characters of Geof and Jo? Try to bring out Geof's concern and Jo's underlying despair. Is this passage typical of the relationship?

Do you agree?

By referring to examples from the text and using the ideas you have found out from the above acting exercises, say if you agree with the critic that the characters have little effect on each other's lives.

The themes of the play

The critic said: 'I doubt very much whether Miss Delaney had any particular theme in mind, anything she wanted to say . . . .'
Maybe, but if not by design she does have something to say about:

Bad mothering   Helen is an appalling mother. She drags her child from one dismal abode to the next around urban Manchester ruining her schooling. She frequently leaves her to go off with her next man. Even the family time of Christmas does not stop her going off. She does not encourage her in any way but puts her down all the time. They talk to each other not like mother and daughter but like two quarrelling sisters.

Single-parent families   Jo is the child of a divorced mother. Her own father was not the man Helen married but a man of very limited ability Helen had a sexual encounter with. Jo lacks the guidance a good father could have given her.

Young love and mixed affairs   In the affair with the coloured boy we see young love with its hopes. Jo is very naive about the boy and his intentions. Helen reveals her prejudice at the end of the play which will not help Jo in any way.

Affairs based on sexual attraction rather than love   Sexual morality is much in the news and always has been a topical subject. Helen goes with men because she likes their wallets and their bodies. There is no suggestion of love in her affair with Peter. She does not set an example to Jo who becomes pregnant by a boy she does not know properly.

Poor housing　The setting of the play is typical of conditions many families have to face who do not have a home of their own. Helen has not schooled Jo in looking after a home caringly and properly. It is left to Geof to produce some homeliness and cleanliness.

Homosexuality　Homosexuals are often poked fun at in stage presentations, whether play or sketch. This play makes the most genuine character a homosexual. It makes us think of Geof as a person with problems. At the end of the play you are upset that Geof is leaving. You feel that he is of more use to Jo than her mother.

Alcoholism　Both Helen and Peter depend on alcohol. We can see how it has ruined both their lives.

Is there a message?

Pick quotations to show how any three of these themes come into the play. Make lists of them under headings. Then decide whether you think Miss Delaney just wanted to tell a story or whether she wanted messages in the play to come across to the audience in a strong way.

Discussions in small groups

1 Could the play have been written in the late 1980s? Does it read as if it is over thirty years old?

2 'It is full of a lingering sadness about the human condition of many people.' Do you agree with this statement or do you find the play mainly comic?

3 What modern themes would you like to see a play about, e.g. nuclear war, animal rights, AIDS, unemployment, education?

4 Discuss these quotations and what you think they imply:

Geof　Anyway I think she's happier here with me than in that dazzling white house . . .

Jo　You know I used to try and hold my mother's hands, but she always used to pull them away from me. So silly really. She had so much love for everyone else, but none for me.

Further study activities

A diary

Write Jo's diary that she keeps after the end of
the play. How does she react to the baby?
Does Helen stay? Does Geof come back? Write
it one entry a week for six weeks.

Write your views

Read this other piece by a critic on a
performance of the play.

Teenagers swept along

The revival of Shelagh Delaney's *A Taste of Honey* which opened at the
Young Vic on February 13 provides an exciting theatrical experience for
that much-neglected sector of the market, the teenage audience. The first-
night teenagers, if a little unnerved by the author's abrupt changes in mood,
were nevertheless swept along by Pam Brighton's bouyant production, to
the extent even of displaying emotion as teddy bear and doll were ill-used
on stage.

Jane Wood as Jo progresses from the innocent who bites off more than
she can chew when she demands to see the photographs in her potential
step-father's wallet, to the knowing sophisticate of the play's end. Lines such
as 'You have been living for forty years' (addressed in incredulous tones to
Helen, her mother), as stressed by Miss Wood, have more force than one
would have thought possible . . .

The Stage, 22 February 1973

How suitable do you think the play is for teenagers? Should there be special
plays for teenagers? Should good plays be enjoyed by all ages? What would
attract you to the theatre? Write down your views.

Consider the title

Use this photograph to consider why the play is
called *A Taste of Honey*. Does it match your
feelings about the relationship that is
represented?

What is happening in the photographs

Here are two stills from the film version of *A Taste of Honey*. What is happening in each? How do the expressions of the characters reveal their feelings? What do you think is being said at the moment the shots were taken?

The world outside the play

The world outside the play is important. You are meant to imagine it in the theatre. But as a film director you could go about Manchester to film. What kind of locations would you seek? Think of the drinking of Helen and Peter; the meetings of Jo and the Boy; Geof shopping; the fair. There is a ship canal in Manchester. How might you use it to add to the atmosphere? What kind of scenery is immediately outside the dismal flat?

Wider reading
Billy Casper and Jo

Billy in *A Kestrel for a Knave* (see Section 2) provides a useful comparison with Jo in *A Taste of Honey*. Compare, for instance, their home conditions and their mothers. How does each find momentary escape, emotional if not physical, from their depressing environment? Do they both develop a resilience through the difficulties of their situations?

Do you think that they will both be survivors, both come through the difficulties of their childhoods to successful adulthood, or have their earlier experiences marked them for life?

If you wished to develop the theme of 'Growing Up in a Hostile Environment' then the following would be good books to read and would provide useful comparisons to Billy and Jo:

> *I know Why the Caged Bird Sings* – Maya Angelou; and
> *Roll of Thunder, Hear My Cry* – Mildred Taylor.

A more direct comparison with Jo's predicament can be seen in *Consequences* by Leonard Kirton (*Scene Scripts Three* – Longman Imprint Books). Another useful book is *Across the Barricades* – Joan Lingard.

4

Cider with Rosie

Laurie Lee

Childhood and growing up

Cider with Rosie is an autobiography, not fiction like a novel but an account of a person's own life. Unlike a novel, it does not have the thread of a story with interacting characters connecting all its parts. It has a different pattern and one with which we are all familiar.

It is about childhood and growing up. We all have these memories and Laurie Lee highlights things we all have in common. The book starts with early childhood, early memories of people, an animal and places which were then strange and sometimes frightening. It goes on to describe going to school and branches out to write about members of his family, neighbours, tales about the neighbourhood and how the changing seasons of the year changed people's habits and activities. For Laurie Lee, one of the most important events in his youth was illness which brought him near to death. He writes about that. He writes about his relations, the entertainment to be had in those days, about his first girl friends and he ends, in his teens, with the first of the family about to leave home to get married.

Besides sharing these experiences so that, if we like, we can compare them with our own, Laurie Lee is presenting us with a world that has disappeared. The village of Slad, not far from Stroud in Gloucestershire, still exists but Laurie Lee is writing about the village as it was fifty or sixty years ago. We are reading about a past that has changed almost out of recognition.

Set in a colourful world of over half a century ago, *Cider with Rosie* is about those occasions that occur in the lives of most of us. What would your youthful autobiography be like?

Your life so far

Think about the story of your life and then write a list of chapter headings for it. Under each heading write a few sentences about what that chapter would contain. Have you moved from place to place? Would each move be given a separate chapter? Will you start with your earliest memories? Will you follow Laurie Lee's example and give a separate chapter to your family or one to winters and summers or one to stories, amusing or serious, about things that have happened to you or to people you know? Has there been for you one outstandingly important event in your life like Laurie Lee's illness?

Comparisons

When you have finished compare your plan of chapter headings and summaries with that taken from *Cider with Rosie* on pages 72 and 73.

Detailed study of the text

Cider with Rosie is more like a book of short stories than a novel and some of its chapters did, in fact, first appear as single articles in magazines. For that reason it seems sensible to deal with it at first chapter by chapter and to ask more general questions about the book later in the section.

If you have already read through the book, you might do the chapter quizzes twice. Answer the questions the first time from memory, then re-read the chapter and answer them again.

First Light

Chapter quiz

1 What was Laurie Lee wrapped up in to protect him from the sun when he rode to his new home in the cart?

2 What interested him about his bedroom ceiling?

3 Why couldn't he see one morning when he woke up?

4 Who had been living in the wood?

5 One night men were drinking and fighting in the pub. What were they celebrating?

Group discussion

How much can members of the group remember about being three years old? What did the world seem like, then? Can individuals remember particular happenings or places or people?
Can some of you remember what it was like to have elder brothers and sisters when you were small? Are there some descriptions in this first chapter where you might say, 'I remember something like that'?

Writing

1 The man who came in from the wood was a deserter from the army. Write a couple of paragraphs as if you were the soldier. You might describe how he came to desert or you might consider how he felt. Was he ashamed at having run away from his regiment? Was he frightened of being arrested? How cold and wet was it in the woods?

2 As if you were one of Laurie Lee's sisters, write your account of the removal day and your impressions of the new house. The girls seem to have been a bit careless and cheerful. Perhaps you enjoyed the upheaval.

Laurie Lee's language

Laurie Lee uses language in an attempt to make his memories read more vividly and colourfully. He may use a single word, peas come in 'long shells of green *pearls*' or a comparison, 'the sun hit me smartly on the face *like a bully*' or a sentence which trots along like his harassed mother. 'All day she trotted to and fro, flushed and garrulous, pouring flowers into every pot and jug she could find on the kitchen floor.' Words, phrases, comparisons, the rhythm of sentences are chosen to add spring and sparkle to what he describes.

Below are two very similar passages. Read both and answer the questions.

A

Then the schoolroom chimney caught on fire. A crowd of sparks went up into the night, carried by the wind and falling afterwards on the road. The blaze in the chimney was noisy and flames came out of the top which seemed to take everything out of the house. I expected to see the whole place on fire. Tiles on the roof were smoking and smoke was coming out of cracks in the chimney, too. We stood in the rain and watched. It seemed a very special sight to us as though someone had arranged for it to happen just on that night.

B

Then the schoolhouse chimney caught on fire. A fountain of sparks shot high into the night, writhing and sweeping on the wind, falling and dancing along the road. The chimney hissed like a firework, great rockets of flame came rushing forth, emptying the tiny house, so that I expected to see chairs and tables, knives and forks, radiant and burning, follow. The moss-tiles smouldered with sulphurous soot, yellow jets of smoke belched from cracks in the chimney. We stood in the rain and watched it entranced, as if the sight had been saved for this day. As if the house had been saved, together with the years's bad litter, to be sent up in flames and rejoicing.

Questions

1 Which passage, A or B, is the one written by Laurie Lee? Don't look before you answer the question but you can check afterwards that you are right by looking at the paragraph that is third from the end of this chapter.

2 Compare the two passages sentence by sentence and, as you do so, write down about five or six words or phrases or comparisons which seem typical of Laurie Lee's lively way of using language.

Descriptions

Here are a few of the ways Laurie Lee attempts a bright description of a thing or person. What is each one about? You can check with the chapter afterwards, if you like.

1 What is this?
'. . . flavoured with sage, coloured with Oxo and laced with a few bones of lamb.'

2 Who are these people?
'. . . like galleons in their busy dresses and I learned the smells and sounds that followed in their wakes, the surge of breath, air of carbolic, song and grumble and smashing of crockery.'

3 Who is this and where does he come from?
'. . . His face was red and crinkled, brilliant like fungus. There were leaves in his mud-matted hair, and leaves and twigs on his crumbling clothes and all over him. His boots were like the black pulp you find when you dig under a tree.'

4 Today we have washing machines and launderettes but you must have seen these sometime. What are they?
'. . . bellying and popping, creaking and whispering, rainbowed with light and winking with a million windows.'

First Names

Chapter quiz

1 What passed the house one night, dragging chains?

2 What might you have seen at Bull's Cross at midnight?

3 Why did the hangman hang himself?

4 How did Cabbage-Stump Charlie use his cabbage stump?

5 What happened in the house when there was a storm and the drain got blocked?

Writing

1 How did they catch the goat? Did Squire Jones recruit a party of men? Did the goat resist, charging them? Did they use a net or ropes or tempt the goat into a pen with food? Write about what might have happened either in the form of a play or as a story.

2 Which is the most interesting scene or event in this chapter? *Either* draw an illustration of it *or* make a rough sketch and explain the sketch in a paragraph *or* describe in words what you would see in the illustration.

3 '. . . dying candles, doors closed on darkness, faces seen upside down, night holes in the ground . . . There were the Old Men, too, who lived in the walls, in floors and down the lavatory; who watched and judged us and were pitilessly spiteful and were obviously gods gone mouldy.'
Write about the things you were afraid of when you were much younger.

Descriptions

Laurie Lee chooses the unusual word to make
his writing more vivid. Write out the following,
picking the one word out of the three given
that you think Laurie Lee would use. [This
exercise might also be done as a discussion.]

And up here, any midnight, but particularly New Year's Eve one could see a

dark		flaring
silver grey	coach drawn by	tired
large		galloping

horses out of control, could

	loud	
hear the	pistol	crack of snapping harness, the screams of passengers, the
	sharp	

breaking		desperate
splintering	of wood and the coachman's	frightened
cracking		loud

cries. The vision

	previous	
recalled some	great	disaster and was rehearsed every night at midnight.
	ancient	

When you have finished, you can compare
your version with the paragraph about the
Bull's Cross Coach in this chapter.

Village School

Chapter quiz

1 Name the two classes in the school.

2 Why did Laurie Lee get into trouble about Vera?

3 Which boy became the hero of the Big Ones and why?

4 Who was 'Fat and Lazy' and who gave him that name?

5 Where did Rosso live and why was he caned?

Discussion

1 When a person left that village school, at that time he had 'nothing in his head more burdensome than a few mnemonics, a jumbled list of wars and a dreamy image of the world's geography' and 'It seemed enough to get by with . . .' That was, of course, over fifty years ago.
When you leave school, what will you carry with you in your head and does that seem enough, 'to get by with' nowadays? (Are there things you think you might safely have missed out and other things you might have learned about?)

2 Laurie Lee remembers 'cutting men out of paper, chalking suns on walls, making snakes from clay' when he was at infant school. Have things changed? What can you remember doing at infant school?

3 Miss Wardley's list of titles for poems is: 'A Kitten. Fairies. My Holidays. An Old Tinker. Charity. Sea Wrack.' What do you think of the list? Could you invent better titles?

Descriptions

1 Where was he and when did this happen?
'Tall girls with frizzled hair and huge boys with sharp elbows began to prod me with hideous interest. They plucked at my scarves, spun me round like a top, screwed my nose and stole my potato.'

2 What does Laurie Lee think this is?
'. . . it was clearly too square to be hair . . .'

3 What did you have to do to make this happen?
'. . . the spit hopped and gambolled like tiny ping pong balls.'

4 Who is this?
'The sight of him squeezed into his tiny desk was worse than a bullock in ballet shoes.'

5 Who is this?
'She wore sharp glass jewellery which winked as she walked and she sounded her "gees" like gongs.'

Writing

1 Write Laurie Lee's School Leaving Report as if you were Miss Wardley.

2 Write about your life as if your were Rosso, the gypsy. Remember you will be writing about life fifty years ago. He may have preferred his hungry, wandering life to being shut up in a house or school.

The Kitchen

Chapter quiz and discussion

In groups of four or five, work out a chapter quiz for this chapter. Pick about five or six questions and then test out other groups. Then, as a class, construct a five question quiz which asks the questions about the most important or most interesting points in the chapter.

Description

In the following passage certain words have been left out. Write the passage, completing it with words of your own. Try to make your description as lively as possible. When you have finished, compare your version and the words you have used with Laurie Lee's choice of words in the paragraph about the kitchen in this chapter.

That kitchen, worn by our boots and lives, was ____, warm and low, whose ____ of furniture seemed never the same but was ____ round each day. A black grate crackled with coal and ____; towels ____ on the guard; the mantel was ____ with fine old china, horse brasses, and freak ____. On the floor were strips of ____ matting, the windows were choked with ____, the walls supported stopped ____ and calendars, and smoky ____ ran over the ceilings.

Writing

1 On one side of the page write the names of Laurie Lee's three half-sisters, the half-brother who lived with them and his two true brothers. Against each write three adjectives used by Laurie Lee to describe them.

2 The last few pages of this chapter describe how the Lee family entertained themselves in the evenings. In what different ways do we spend our evenings now? Write a brief account of the differences that have taken place in our lives.

Grannies in the Wainscot

Chapter quiz

1 Which Granny was 'Er-Down-Under'?
2 Whose bun of hair when it had been combed and set looked like a 'small shining ball of snow'?
3 How did Granny Trill's father die?
4 How many hours did Granny Trill stay with him?
5 What was Granny Trill's vice?
6 How old was Granny Wallon when Granny Trill died?

Descriptions

1 What made them feel like this?

   '. . . a curious rocking would seize the head; tides rose from our feet like a fever, the kitchen walls began to shudder and shift . . .'

2 Who are these?

   'They looked like starlings, flecked with jet, and they walked in a tinkle of darkness.'

3 What is this?

   'Reeking substance of the underworld, clay-brown dust of decay, of powdered flesh and crushed old bones, rust scrapings and the rubbish of graves.'

Language

Laurie Lee describes Granny Wallon's ingredients for her wine by the way they smell, 'the sharp, spiced honey of those cowslips', 'the coppery reeking dandelion', 'the bitter poppy's whiff of powder', 'the cat's breath . . . elder'.
Choose one of these and write about it in terms of the scents and smells you will notice there.

Preparing something to bake or cook
Inside a shop, a railway or bus station or an
   open air market
A summer garden

Writing

Had the grannies been married? Had they always lived in the same house or had they moved there? Had they worked as servants or in a shop or on a farm? Write a short account of the life of one of them.

Public Death, Private Murder

Chapter quiz

1 Who was Vincent?
2 What played tunes for eerie Miss Flynn among her apple trees?
3 Who found her body?
4 In what season of the year were there most suicides?
5 Apart from old age, what killed Hannah and Joseph?

Discussion

Are old people looked after better nowadays than they were in those times?

Descriptions

1 Where is this place and how had the milk come there?

   '. . . flat and green and empty, and a smudge of milk clung to the reeds.'

2 What made old people in the village curl 'up like salted snails'?

3 Who are these?

   '. . . they resembled two tawny insects, slow but deft in their movements; a little foraging, some frugal feeding, then any amount of stillness.'

Language

'We liked her too in an eerie way . . .'

Write down about five or six of the words or phrases which help to build up this 'eeriness' of Miss Flynn.

Writing

Write down as conversation or as a play what was said between the 'dark-suited stranger' or policeman when he came to interview the dying old lady about the watch and the death of Vincent ten years before.

Laurie Lee's mother and great-grandmother

64

Mother

Chapter quiz

1 What was the mother's worst subject at school?

2 What was her first job?

3 Name the pub she worked in.

4 How did she meet Laurie Lee's father?

5 What did she like collecting?

Writing

1 You start work as a maid servant in a big house about the time Laurie Lee's mother started work, about 70 or 80 years ago. You could write as if you were the mother. Write a letter to a friend, describing what you have to do, some of the people, the butler, the cook, the other servants you work with and how you feel about it.

2 In play form or as conversation write the interview that took place between the mother and Laurie Lee's father when she came to apply for the job as his housekeeper.

Winter and Summer

Chapter quiz

1 How did the boys keep their hands warm on a winter's day?

2 What was the name of the farmer they helped?

3 Who quarrelled with the carol singers and went off to sing alone?

4 Where in summer did they play cricket?

5 What running game did they play on summer nights?

Comparisons

Laurie Lee's comparisons seem designed to give you the feeling or picture of something as exactly as possible. Pick out the similes he has used by looking at the following and answering the questions.

1 Which comparison, a), b) or c) gives most clearly the sharp, jabbing, tingling feeling of chilblains?

'poor little Phyllis sat rocking in a chair holding her chilblains
a) like a handful of pain
b) like a handful of bees
c) like a handful of stones

2 Which suggests the sting of frosty air?

'when we breathed the air, it smelt
a) like frost
b) like fog
c) like needles

3 Which gives you the picture of a dog in foggy frost, surrounded by the mist of its breath?

'a dog trotted past like a
a) sigh in the night
b) a ghost in a cloud
c) a shadow on a wall

Language

Find the paragraph beginning, 'We sat by the roadside and scooped the dust with our hands and made little piles in the gutters.' It is about five pages from the end of the chapter. Read it through and then write as vividly as you can a description of things heard, seen and felt on a winter day.

When you have finished, compare what you have imagined with the paragraph beginning, 'Now the winter's day was set in motion and we rode through its crystal kingdom.' It is about three pages from the beginning of the chapter.

Sick Boy

Descriptions

1 When Laurie Lee felt, 'a swaying in the head and lungs full of pulsing thorns' what did he know was going to happen?

2 When he was ill what began 'to bulge and ripple and roar, to flap like pastry, melt like sugar and run bleeding with hideous hues'?

3 When he was getting better, what seemed like 'milk of paradise; it came through the windows in beaming tides, in currents of green and blue, bearing debris of birdsong, petals, voices . . .'?

4 After that who would come, 'carolling upstairs with . . . breakfast, bright as a windblown lark'?

Writing

Laurie Lee writes about the stages of first feeling ill, then the discomfort of actually being ill, feeling even worse and then getting better. Write about one of these things in a paragraph or two, choosing the language carefully so that the reader can share your feelings vividly.

The Uncles

Uncles

On one side of the page write down the first names of Laurie Lee's uncles, including his great uncle. Against each, when the information is given in the chapter, write the name of his wife and the job he had.

Descriptions

1 Laurie Lee's Auntie Minnie was 'a tiny, pretty, parted-down-the-middle woman'. What does the phrase 'parted-down-the-middle' tell you about her character?

2 When Uncle Sid 'came in to bat men covered their heads and retired piecemeal to the boundaries.' What kind of a batsman was he?

3 Laurie Lee remembers all his uncles as being like 'a ring of squat megaliths on some local hill, bruised by weather and scarred with old glories.' What does that suggest about their size, the colour of their faces and their past histories?

Writing

1 Which of the uncles do you find most interesting? Write your own account of him, pointing out the things about him that interest you.

2 Do you have an aunt, uncle or other relation who seems to you to be, like one of Laurie Lee's uncles, a bit larger than life and memorable? Write an account of that person.

Outings and Festivals

Chapter quiz

In groups work out a list of about five or six questions on this chapter. These mini-quizzes could then be tried out among groups. If, however, you supply the answers, this could become a team game with the quizmaster editing out any questions duplicated by the individual groups.

Radio commentary

Using details from the paragraphs in the book, write a radio commentary on the Peace Day Procession. (Why would such a broadcast not have been possible at the time?)

Procession arriving at the squire's house

Poster

Design a poster, using the paragraphs in this chapter, to advertise the concert that took place after the Parochial Church Tea. List the performers and their acts.

Comparisons

1 '. . . Thirteen-year-old Phyllis . . . skipped *like a magpie* around her.'
   What colour was Phyllis's fancy dress?

2 '. . . I tuned up *like an ape threading needles.*'
   What does that suggest about the way he did his tuning?

3 '. . . far out on the rippled mud a white pier *like a sleeping dragon.*'
   In what way or ways might the pier have been similar to a dragon?

Language

Below the following passage you are given a choice of two words to be used in each of the gaps. Write out the passage choosing, in each case, the word that you think Laurie Lee would have used. You can check your version afterwards with the paragraph in the book.

Night odours come _____ from woods and gardens; _____ musks and sharp green _____. In the sky the _____ stars _____ up and down, rhythmically, as we _____ along. Glow worms, brighter than lamps or candles, spike the fields with their _____ fires, while huge horned beetles _____ out of the dark and _____ blindly around our heads.

drifting/rushing   thick/sweet   smells/acids
bright/fat   bounce/shine   trudge/walk
bright/lemon   stumble/come   fly/buzz

First Bite at the Apple

The girls

1 Which girl was short, plump, about sixteen with 'large blue-bottle eyes' and 'daft about religion'?

2 Which girl was big for an eleven-year-old, shabbily blonde and had eyes 'drowsy with insolence.'?

3 Which girl was thin with brushed-back hair, a 'cool face' and 'speechless grace'?

4 Which girl was devious and had 'sharp salts of wickedness on her' and looked at you with the 'sly glittering eyes of her mother'?

Language – for discussion

In each of the gaps in the following a choice of three words is given. Discuss which would be the most effective, striking and lively word to use and then compare your version with Laurie Lee's. You will find the paragraph at the end of the 'Rosie' episode.

There was something about that evening which (wakens/stirs/dilates) the memory even now. The long hills (roared/rippled/slavered) like Chinese dragons, crimson in the setting sun. The (uneven/shifting/pebbly) lane (lassoed/caught/hindered) my feet and tried to trip me up. And the lake, as we passed it, rose (choppy/hissing/splashing) with waves and tried to drown us among its cannibal fish.

Writing

The cider drinking with Rosie is obviously important enough to Laurie Lee for him to make it the title of the book. Do you think he is right? Or would some other title fit the book better? Say why you think *Cider with Rosie* is a good title or, if not, explain why another title you have chosen is better.

Last Days

Eating out

In short phrases like these describe what happened at a picnic or a barbecue or any other meal in the open. Notice how Laurie Lee makes a kind of list, how he uses an unusual adverb 'the fire smoked glumly' or simile 'the young men sat . . . like martyrs' and how he ends with something no one really expected or wanted. Your version could be real or imaginary, pleasant or unpleasant. Don't write more than a paragraph.

'We were ordered to scatter and gather sticks and to build a fire for the kettle. The fire smoked glumly and stung our eyes, the young men sat round like martyrs, the milk turned sour, the butter fried on the bread, cake crumbs got stuck to the cucumber, wasps seized the treacle, the kettle wouldn't boil and we ended by drinking the jellies.'

Changes

1 When Laurie Lee was a boy of about two what was the fastest way people in his village could travel?

2 What sort of tyres did the first buses have?

3 What is a 'Collect' and where will you find it?

4 How was the organ in the village church operated?

5 Which festival did Laurie Lee like best?

6 What did the squire's Big House become?

7 How did the girls' boyfriends travel when they came to do their courting?

8 For entertainment what did people start to have instead of 'flutes and cornets', 'wind harps' and 'gramophones with horns'?

Now write an account of some of the social and other changes in such things as transport, church-going and technology that have taken place since the time of *Cider with Rosie*. You can use the answers you gave to the quiz and add other ideas of your own.

Sunday

Laurie Lee says that Sundays were a 'combination of indulgence and discipline'. In what ways did people have a good time on Sundays and in what ways were they made to do things and conform?

Further study activities

A family tree

Construct a family tree for Laurie Lee showing all his relations from grandfather down.

A news item

Write the news item, complete with headline about one of these things:

1 The end of the Great War in the village *or* how it was celebrated in another town. (You could do some research in a library for an account of this second topic.)

2 A 'human interest' story about Joseph and Hannah Brown in the chapter, 'Public Death, Private Murder' and the way they were put into the workhouse.

3 An account of a cricket match in which Sid, one of the uncles in the chapter 'The Uncles', played.

A video

You are making a video tape of one of the characters in the book. Pick the character you wish to feature, describe what scenes you would use and write the interview you might have with the person.

Study the language

Which of the passages on page 70, A or B, was written by Laurie Lee? Explain, without looking the passage up, how you know. Illustrate your answer with quotations from one or both passages.

A

The noise of the mower came to us across the field, rabbits jumped like mad all over the place and the hay smelt nice and fresh. The farmer's men were all hard at work getting in the hay. Tall, whiskered men lifted the dried grass, their chests all hairy. The air whizzed as they forked and the hay went up like feathers on top of the wagons.

B

The whirr of the mower met us across the stubble, rabbits jumped like firecrackers across the fields and the hay smelt crisp and sweet. The farmer's men were all hard at work, raking, turning and loading. Tall, whiskered fellows forked the grass, their chests like bramble patches. The air swung with their forks and the swathes took wing and rose like eagles to the tops of the wagons.

Writing

1 On one side of a page list as many as you can of the ways in which Laurie Lee spent his leisure time, inside and outside the house. On the other side of the page, list all your leisure activities nowadays.

2 'Laurie Lee does not paint a sweet and sentimental picture of life in Slad. He includes the darker and sadder side of his past life there.' Do you agree or not? Illustrate your answer by describing things in the book that have influenced your opinion.

3 Was Laurie Lee's childhood happier and more interesting than childhood today? Give your opinion, describing things in the book and in reality that show why you think as you do.

4 Pick a scene or incident in the book that has impressed you and show how Laurie Lee's use of language has made it more interesting.

5 In what ways do you think this picture (opposite) suggests the atmosphere, setting, characters and tone of *Cider with Rosie*?

Chapter headings and brief summaries

(refer back to page 56, 'Comparisons')

First Light
Tells of removal day to their new home, some of Laurie Lee's earliest memories, a deserter from the army who lives in the woods and the day the Great War ended.

First Names
Laurie Lee, about three years old, remembers a frightening goat, a ghostly coach, a hangman, various odd people who lived in or around the village and a night of storm and flood.

Village School
He goes unwillingly to school and hits a little girl. He remembers the first bad-tempered Head Teacher and how she is lifted on to a cupboard by a boy. He writes about fights, getting out of school and a gipsy boy.

The Kitchen
He mentions his father who did not live with them and describes his half sisters, his brothers and life in the house which centred on the kitchen; the meals, the fire, his violin and conversations.

Grannies in the Wainscot
They shared the house with two old ladies, Granny Trill and Granny Wallon who disliked each other. Granny Wallon made wine, Granny Trill sat still, read her almanac and told tales of her woodsman father. When Granny Trill died of a broken hip, Granny Wallon died soon afterwards.

Public Death, Private Murder
A gang of village youths murder Vincent, a boastful villager returned from New Zealand. The beautiful Miss Flynn commits suicide. Mr Davies takes to his bed for the last time. Hannah and Joseph Brown have to go to the workhouse where they die.

Mother
This describes her life as a servant in a big house, her work in a pub and as a housekeeper and her slapdash, loveable character.

Winter and Summer
Tells of the activities, skating, carol singing in winter and the activities carried on in the summer months.

Sick Boy
This is about Laurie Lee's sickly babyhood and the many serious illnesses he suffered during the rest of his boyhood.

The Uncles
Gives a series of brief, thumbnail sketches of Laurie Lee's various memorable uncles and the lives they led.

Outings and Festivals
This recollects the fancy dress parade on Peace Day 1919, a seaside outing and the feast and entertainment in January at the Parochial Church Tea.

First Bite at the Apple
In this Laurie Lee remembers various girl friends that he knew as he became adolescent and contains the incident when he drank cider with Rosie.

Last Days
He takes a final look back on life in Slad and writes about the changes that are beginning to take place.

Wider reading

Two years before *Cider with Rosie* first appeared, Keith Waterhouse's recollections of his childhood in an urban environment were published.

Read the extract on pages 74 to 76. What similarities and differences are there between the characters? Does Waterhouse's account reflect any of your own childhood experiences?

Many authors have written about their childhood experiences. 'Childhood Experiences' would be an interesting theme to follow. Also read:

Boy – Roald Dahl;
Blue Remembered Hills – Rosemary Sutcliff;
Black Boy – Richard Wright;
A Northern Childhood – George Layton;
Joby – Stan Barstow;
Our Lives – ILEA English Centre.

The following are more difficult to read but are about girls growing up:

A Long Way to Verona – Jane Gardam;
Lark Rise to Candleford – E. V. Thompson (which is a true story like *Cider with Rosie*).

Recollections of childhood

'Have we to play truth or dare?' said Kathleen after a bit.

I didn't like truth or dare. Sooner or later it always got round to who goes out with who and kissing and that. I never said 'dare' in this game. I always said 'truth'.

'Truth or dare?' said Kathleen.

'Truth,' said Barbara Monoghan.

'Errrm – how many times have you been out with Big Rayner?'

'What, by himself?'

'Yer,' said Kathleen.

'Errr – once to the Tivoli one Saturday afternoon, once down to Clarkson's woods. No, twice. Three times, altogether,' said Barbara.

I was looking over at the fence where Marion and Big Rayner had gone, but I could not see them any more. This was the first time I had ever seen them together. Marion always said she didn't like the big lads, and I know her mother had told her to keep away from Big Rayner.

She was wearing her velvet dress, the one that looked like our tablecloth. It wasn't a very nice *dress*, because it was all old and bits of the velvet had worn off, but I liked it because you always think of somebody in a certain thing and I always thought of Marion in this velvet dress. Not the night before but the night before that we had made some furniture out of old matchboxes in their house, using drawing pins for the drawer handles. Marion hadn't seemed much interested.

'Truth or dare?' said Barbara Monoghan.

'Truth,' said Kathleen.

'No, dare,' said Barbara.

'No, truth. You had truth so I'm having truth.'

'How many times have you been in the tusky fields with our kid?' said Barbara Monoghan.

'Aw, not answering that,' said Kathleen.

'Well dare, then.'

'All right, dare.'

'Dare you to ask *him* something.' Barbara Monoghan nodded towards me and began whispering in Kathleen's ear. They both started giggling. I started peeling the veins off a rhubarb leaf and pretended not to take any notice.

'Truth or dare,' said Kathleen Fawcett.

'Truth' I said.

'Well what – kkkkkksh!' She made a lot of giggly false starts before she asked the question that Barbara Monoghan had whispered to her. 'What colour knick-knacks does Marion Longbottom wear?'

Only Barbara could think up a question like that.

'Blue,' I guessed. I thought they *meant* me to guess.

'Ha, he knows!' shouted Barbara Monoghan. 'Huh, *I'll* tell, don't you worry!' she cackled.

'Ask him how he knows,' said Kathleen Fawcett.

'I-I-I was only guessing,' I said. I could feel myself going red.

'Yer, bet you were!' said Barbara. 'What colour ones does Kathleen Fawcett wear, then?'

'Oo, Barbara Monoghan!' said Kathleen. I was trying hard for some excuse to get away. Barbara Monoghan started pulling her dress up and pulling it back again, very quickly, over her knees, with Kathleen shouting: 'Blue! Brown!' It was the kind of stupid thing they were always doing.

'Truth or dare,' said Barbara Monoghan, when she had finished acting about.

'I've had it once!' I went.

'Ah, well, you've got to have another. Truth or dare?'

'Dare,' I said. I couldn't say truth again.

'Dare you to kiss Kathleen Fawcett.'

'Oo, you wait, Barbara Monoghan!' said Kathleen. I didn't know what to do. I didn't want to kiss Kathleen Fawcett, and the way she had said: 'Oo, you wait!' to Barbara made me think she didn't want me to. But if I didn't they would laugh at me. I suddenly drew in my breath and said: 'Listen!' in a hoarse voice.

'What's up?'

'My Aunt Betty's shouting me.'

'Caw, trying to get out of it!' cried Barbara Monoghan.

'No, listen!' I stood up and cupped my hands to my face and shouted: 'Just coming!' across the fields. 'I can't hear nobody,' said Kathleen. 'Want to wash your ears out, then,' I said. 'They're sprouting cabbages.'

I set off through the rhubarb leaves with Barbara and Kathleen shouting after me: 'We'll tell Mrs Longbottom! Tea-cher's pe-et! You wait!'

'And you needn't go to our kid's fire!' shouted Barbara Monoghan. I could still smell the wood smoke, so it must have been Mono's fire in their garden.

'I'm not off to it. My Auntie Betty wants me!' I shouted back.

'Yer, bet she does!' called Kathleen Fawcett.

I went back through Theaker's garden and into Coronation Grove. The wood smell was very strong there and I walked up the street as far as Mono's. I stood by their gate for a few seconds and then walked into the garden and along the side path to the back garden.

They were all sitting on bricks round a fire, melting lead from some piping they had pinched and moulding it into squares in an old Oxo tin. My heart sank because Ted and Raymond Garnett were there, besides Mono, Little Rayner and a few more.

As I walked over towards them Little Rayner started singing: 'Here comes the bride, fifty inches wide!' Raymond Garnett said nothing. Mono stood up and said: 'Who told you you could come in?'

I said: 'Nobody.' It was a law that you could go in anybody's garden if they had a fire.

'Do you want another fight, or something?' asked Little Rayner. I didn't reply, but stood on the fringe of the fire.

'Cos I'll give you one if you do,' said Little Rayner. He was small and thin, not like their kid, and he never fought anybody.

'*He-e* couldn't knock the skin off a rice pudding,' said Ted.

'Have we to set on him?' said Little Rayner.

'Cuh, seven against one!' I said.

'We'll take you on one at a time if you want,' said Raymond Garnett. It was the first time he had spoken. He had changed in his voice. He sounded sure of himself and his voice had got the harsh rasp of Mono and Big Rayner to it now.

Little Rayner picked up a stone and held it up ready to throw.

'Dance!' he said.

'You throw that if you dare!' I said.

'Why, what will you do?' asked Mono mockingly.

'Dance!' said Little Rayner.

He threw the pebble at my feet and picked up another. Ted picked up a piece of slate and joined in. 'Dance!' he said. Nearly all of them had stones. I had to jump up and down to get out of the way of the stones that they were lobbing at my ankles.

'Gi-ive over?' I shouted. 'Lay off!'

'Go down to Uncle Mad's and he'll kiss you better!' said Ted. 'Won't he, Garno?'

'Don't *you* start!' said Raymond Garnett.

Mono came up to me and started pushing at me with his elbows.

'Go on, scram!' he said.

'Won't if I don't want to,' I said.

'*Ho-op* it, college cad!' shouted Ted.

'Cur, just cos I got ten out of ten in composition!' I sneered back at him. Me and Ted had always been rivals in composition. We had to write a composition about a day in the life of a sheep, and I had written it as though I was the sheep and I got ten out of ten.

'*Ho-op* it, wolf cub!' said Mono.

'Yer, well I'm not in the boy sprouts like some people,' I said.

Little Rayner put up his two fingers in a mock salute. 'I promise to do my best!' he went in a squeaking voice. He had been chucked out of the wolf cubs.

'Dance!' said Ted. I turned round and walked out of the garden. Little Rayner sang after me: 'Here comes the bride, fifty inches wide!' 'No this is it,' I heard Raymond Garnett say. 'Here comes the bride, with a bla-ack eye!'

I walked down Coronation Grove, feeling my split lip swollen and numb. Near the end of our street I began to straighten my back and hold my arms at my sides, curving my fingers a bit, like Big Rayner did. I pushed out my split lip and glared round me.

from *There is a Happy Land* by Keith Waterhouse (Longman Imprint Books)

5

Gregory's Girl

Bill Forsyth

This has to be the match of the day.

Gregory's Girl A

Introduction to the play script

The play script is adapted from Bill Forsyth's Scottish film. It differs in several ways, but the main storyline is kept intact, that of Gregory, the adolescent, and his love for Dorothy, the star of the first eleven football team in a comprehensive school. It suffers from having to put everything into short scenes, for example, Scene 3 is just two and a half pages. There are thirteen scenes in all. Therefore, it does not have the dramatic effect of a play with acts. J. B. Priestley in *An Inspector Calls* skilfully uses his acts and their endings for dramatic tension. Harold Brighouse uses his for surprise and comic effect in *Hobson's Choice*. But the play script of *Gregory's Girl* does have the freshness of the film.

What it lacks is the scenery that the camera in a film can show us. We are not always sure where the play is set. In Scene 2, for instance, nobody says they are outside a nurse's home.

Setting and situation

Read this short scene from *The Homecoming* by Harold Pinter. The stage directions have been missed out, but you hardly need them. Make a list of the things you know about the setting and the situation simply from the conversation of Teddy and Ruth.

Teddy	Well, the key worked. They haven't changed the lock.
Ruth	No one's here.
Teddy	They're in bed.
Ruth	Can I sit down?
Teddy	Of course, sit there. That's my father's chair.
Ruth	That one?
Teddy	Yes, that's it. I'll pop up and check my room's still there.
Ruth	It can't have moved.
Teddy	No, I mean see if my bed's still there.
Ruth	Shouldn't we wake someone up? Tell them you're here?
Teddy	Not at this time of night. It's too late. Anyway, I think I can hear them snoring. What do you think of the room? Big, isn't it? It's a big house. Actually, there was a wall there . . . we knocked it down . . . years ago, before I went to America . . . to make an open living area. Let's just go to bed. See them all in the morning. . . . see my father . . . he's dying to meet my wife.
Ruth	How long will we stay?
Teddy	A few days.

Set the scene

Add some lines for the actors so that the audience know where they are for Scenes 1, 2, 4, 8 and 14 of *Gregory's Girl*. Think also about what they might say about the weather for the outside scenes. Madeline might begin Scene 1 by saying: 'It's cold out here on the field.'

Then imagine that you are a scenic designer. Design your set with the goal-posts and then design what bits of scenery you would have for each scene. How would you suggest Gregory's home or the shopping centre, for instance? You cannot have a lot of heavy or large scenery because you must keep the play moving without pauses for big scene changes. As it would be hopeless with so many scenes to have constant changes, you could also work into the above simple props or additions to costume that might show or symbolise the change of scene. Use both plans and descriptions of what you want.

Young love

In *Gregory's Girl* the author tries to make the conflicts and problems of young love as realistic as possible. The dialogue is real too. Gregory tells us:

'I'm in love. I can't eat. I'm awake half the night, when I think about it I feel dizzy. I'm restless – it's wonderful.'

Writing

Write down in what ways this play is about young love. How do the characters – not just Gregory – react to the strong feelings inside them? Use quotations to show how they feel. What problems do they have in their love and friendships with the opposite sex?

The role of Madeline

Madeline acts as a kind of commentator on Gregory's feelings. She knows exactly what is happening to him better than he does himself. Madeline is only about ten but she is an amusing character creation as she has the mind of a very mature person. Much humour was extracted from her and Richard in the film. Study what Madeline says:

'He wants to impress. Make an impression on the girls. Trouble is he can't play football to save his life.'

'She's very attractive . . . I knew you would fall for that type.'

'Talk to Dorothy . . . ask her out . . . she won't say no, I'll bet you . . . but don't treat her too special . . . if you're too romantic it could scare a girl off.'

Discussion

How accurate a judge of Gregory is Madeline? Is she oversmart for her age? In a realistic play is she far-fetched? How do she and Richard handle Gregory?

Write about the characters

Write about the roles of Gregory and Dorothy. Use as many quotes as you can. Then write how you feel Madeline fits into this love story. Say how real you think the author has made these characters. How do the pictures opposite show the relationship between the two?

Realistic dialogue

In the previous section we said that the play was realistic. It is about real life — teenage love — and is set in a modern housing estate. In the film the actors wore contemporary fashions.

Grange Hill is a realistic drama TV series of school life in a London comprehensive school. Look at this piece of dialogue from it:

> (*Tucker, Alan, Benny and Hughes are making their way back to class.*)

Alan	You don't 'arf take some chances, Tucker.
Tucker	It was the truth, wasn't it?
Simon	Only just. But I'm still in it for bunking off.
Tucker	So am I. But it's better than being done for the other thing. [They have set part of the school on fire.]
Hughes	I thought you said you never came back last night?
Tucker	Who said we did? That Caretaker hates me. He'd get me done for anything if he could . . . . which reminds me. You never went up the tower. Right, men? He can do it at lunchtime.
Alan	You're joking, aren't you?
Tucker	Flippin' 'eck. You're not chicken, are you?
Alan	I am.
Simon	So am I. Anyway, I won't be here at dinner time. I want to go and see somebody.
Alan	See you at dinner, Tucker. I'm going to History.
Tucker	See you, Alan. What do we have now? (*Simon reaches for his timetable card*)
Simon	Bloomin 'eck, I've lost my timetable card again.

Compare the dialogue

Compare this piece of dialogue with any page of dialogue in the school or on the field in *Gregory's Girl*. Do you find one any more like real life speech than the other? Does *Gregory's Girl* need more slang? In real life people hesitate a lot. They use 'ums' and 'ers' a great deal; they pause frequently. Why might this not always be suitable for plays? Write a piece of dialogue that happened in your school this week or improvise (as a play) what happened and then write it down as dialogue.

NB: Much of *Gregory's Girl* was made from improvisation done by young actors.

Gregory – a character profile

The main character in the play is Gregory. What are his problems? What are his hopes? What is he worried about? How is his growing-up affecting him? What is his relationship with his parents? What is his relationship with his sister? How does he relate to other pupils in the school? How does he get on with his teachers? How does he handle his affair with Dorothy and later Susan?

Write a character profile

Build up a character profile of Gregory by writing reports on him by these people:

Madeline
Gregory's father
Miss Ford (assume she is his form teacher)
Dorothy
Susan
Phil

Sex in the play

Much of the play is about the obsession young people have with the bodies of the opposite sex:

Gregory   .... she's got long lovely hair, she always looks really clean and fresh, and she smells ... mmm ... lovely. Even if you just pass her in the corridor she smells ... mmm, gorgeous ... She's got teeth, lovely teeth, lovely white, white teeth .....

Read scene 2 and 8, for example.

Discussion

How does the play bring out typical obsessions of teenagers? (Not just sex – Steve, for instance, is obsessed by cooking.) How true to life is it compared with your school? Should there be sex talk to make it realistic or would this spoil it as a play? Has the play dated at all in its attitudes to teenage sexual behaviour? Is there any difference between what teenagers say and do, in your experience?

The girls in the play

The girls in the play are more mature than the boys and thus more in control of things. Improvise the scene, in groups of four, in which Dorothy, Susan, Margo and Carol plan Gregory's night out.

Write a play scene

Write out your improvisation as a play scene. Add to this how real you find the girl characters in the play. Are they more real than those of a love story in a teenage magazine? What do you think of Dorothy's love of football?

Further study activities

A film is divided up into several types of shot: a close-up (see the top photograph on page 81), a medium shot (see the bottom photograph on page 81), a long shot (a distance picture going as far as the eye can see). Take part of Scene 14, e.g. the scene with Susan, and write down what shots you would use, if you were a film director. Remember you must not stay on any one shot too long or the audience will get bored.

Write a scene as fiction

Write Scene 3 as if it was part of a novel. Be sure to compose narrative links and write good descriptions of the characters. You will have to decide what dialogue to keep in your composition.

Wider reading

The attraction of *Gregory's Girl* is its contemporary feel, that it has hit some aspect of modern girl/boy relationships. Compare it with:

'Seeing Beauty Queen Home' – Bill Naughton (a short story from *Late Night on Watling Street*);
'The Ragman's Daughter' – Alan Sillitoe (a short story from *A Sillitoe Selection*).

The Experience of Love (another book in the Longman Imprint series) will provide other useful comparisons, particularly as it includes poetry (which you should not neglect in your wider reading), as will *Across the Barricades* by Joan Lingard (also another modern love story).

Animal Farm

George Orwell

Introduction to fable

Stories in which animals speak and behave like human beings are called fables or apologues. Aesop, a wise slave in ancient Greece, wrote fables which suggested that human beings could sometimes be as stupid as donkeys or as careless and feckless as grasshoppers. Slaves in nineteenth-century America told tales in which a rabbit who, like themselves, was powerless but clever, always got the better of a fox who, like a slave owner, was powerful but stupid. A man called Joel Chandler Harris collected these tales and published them as the stories of Brer Rabbit and Brer Fox.

More recently Richard Adams has written books in which most of the characters are talking rabbits or talking dogs. You must, too, have seen Disney cartoon versions of books in which the characters are animals with human characteristics.

Satire

Satire is used by a writer to show us how foolish or greedy or cruel human beings can be. The writer hopes that his satirical picture of human awfulness will arouse our amusement and contempt. We may learn a lesson and, perhaps, avoid such evils ourselves. You can see how useful an animal fable can be as satire. A fable can suggest that some people are as mindless as sheep or as greedy as pigs or as savage as wild dogs. If these facts are simply and crudely stated, readers might feel insulted. They could be annoyed rather than amused. If the facts are put in the form of a fable about animals they are suggested more mildly and subtly. Presented like that they can be more persuasive.

History

George Orwell based *Animal Farm* on events which followed the Russian Revolution of 1917. That revolution turned Russia, ruled by an emperor, into a communist state. Communism was founded on the ideas of Karl Marx whose book, *Das Capital* suggests that it is fairer and more just if workers rather than the rich rule a country. Lenin led the revolution and, after his death, there was a struggle for power between Stalin and Trotsky. Stalin won and Trotsky had to escape from Russia in disgrace. Stalin took over total power, setting up his own secret police and killing or imprisoning those who criticised him or stood in his way.

In 1941, Hitler, an equally evil tyrant, had been in power in Germany for some time. In Britain, Winston Churchill was Prime Minister. Stalin signed a peace treaty with Hitler but it was soon broken and Germany invaded Russia. You may be able to recognise which of the animals is most like Stalin.

Hitler was a grasping ruler, treacherous and deceitful, always eager to extend his territory. Churchill, a more humane politician, since Britain was already at war with Germany, sent help to Russia. You may be able to decide which of the farmers whose land joins Animal Farm is most like Hitler and which most like Churchill.

Not knowing much about the Russian Revolution or the Second World War will, however, not spoil your understanding or enjoyment of *Animal Farm*.

Detailed study of the text

Review as you read

As you read the book, make your own assessment of it, chapter by chapter. Set out your 'log' like this. Draw three lines down a page of your book, spacing them as we have done below. In your first column write the number of the chapter. In the second write a title you have made up yourself for that chapter. In the third column write in note form a brief description of what the chapter has been about. In the fourth write your own opinion of the chapter. Your 'Chapter Review' or 'Chapter Log' should look like this.

Chapter	Title	Story	Opinion
1	On Animal Farm	Introduces animals. Major's speech.	Animals interesting. Too much speech by Major. Could be more action.
2			
3			

The beginning of the book

The full length animated cartoon

You are making a cartoon film of *Animal Farm*. Prepare for it by making notes on what each character should look like as you go through the earlier chapters of the book. You will have to advise your animators and illustrators on how they should draw each character.

Write down the name of each person or animal, say what kind of animal it is and make a note of what expression it should have. One line each should be enough, like this:

> Jones: farmer – heavy drinker, bad-tempered
>
> Major: large pig – old, wise, kindly, likes making speeches

(If your school has the facilities, you could compare your ideas with those depicted in the original full length animated cartoon of *Animal Farm*.)

If you are a good artist yourself, you could make your own sketches, labelled with names, and ask other people to comment on your work.

Discussion

Is Major right? Could farm and tame animals manage to live without the help of human beings? Would wild animals live safer and better lives without human beings? How dependent on animals are we human beings and how dependent on us are they?

Chapter 2

Write a letter

You are a farm-worker. You have just started work on Jones's farm a week or two before the animals' rebellion. Write a letter to a friend, telling him or her just how easy or hard you find the work and what you think of Mr Jones.

A TV interview

Mr Jones talks to a local TV station about what happened when he was driven out. Write down what he says either in play-form as an interview with someone or as a speech direct to camera. Remember he would know nothing of the animals' plans and would have to guess why the animals behaved as they did. Don't forget that he would be angry. Would he demand help from the local council or the police?

Sugarcandy Mountain

Moses, because he likes such things, describes the ravens' heaven as a place of lump sugar and linseed cake. What sort of heaven might another animal imagine? Choose an animal, choose that animal's name for its heaven and write about the place as if you were that animal.

Chapter 3

Warning signs

What do the pigs do in this chapter which suggest that they intend to turn the animal revolution to their own advantage?

Quick quiz

How many words would Boxer be able to read? Write them down.

Chapter 4

News commentary

You are a reporter, either for radio or television. (For television, the viewers will be able to see what happens. You will have to explain rather than describe.) Write, as an eye-witness, a commentary on the attack on the farm. This activity will help to prepare you for the role play which follows.

Role play

For this you will need to pick two interviewers, one to interview each side in the battle, and people to represent the following; Mr Jones, one of Mr Jones's men, the stable lad, Snowball, Boxer, the Cat, a goose. Then act out, in character, your version of what happened in the battle. You may like to discuss first whether those interviewed would tell the simple truth, or boast, or complain that the other side had taken unfair advantage and so on, according to their character. Would Boxer, for instance, boast? Would the Cat?

Chapter 5

Writing

1 In the form of a play, write the arguments that go on between Napoleon and Snowball about how they think the farm should be defended. You could have other pigs such as Squealer, Minimus and some whose names you can invent, joining in the argument on both sides.

2 You are Snowball after his escape from Animal Farm. How do you feel? Bitter, angry and wanting revenge, perhaps? You take refuge on another farm and tell the other pigs your story. Write down what Snowball might say about the events, starting from the revolution, that have taken place.

Chapter 6

Writing

1 How many of the commandments, listed in Chapter 2, have been broken at this stage in the book? Who has broken them and in what way?

Looking at the truth

Discuss the way in which the pigs twist the truth so that it always looks as if they are acting unselfishly and for the good of others. The last paragraphs of Chapter 3 give an example. How is the truth twisted to show that Napoleon is the true protector of Animal Farm and Snowball the enemy?
In the last paragraph of Chapter 6, who really made the pig tracks on the knoll near the windmill? Why might they seem to lead toward Foxwood farm?

Chapter 7

Writing

1 'Whenever anything went wrong it became usual to attribute it to Snowball.'
Explain why it would be useful to the other pigs to have someone to blame for things that went wrong on the farm.

2 Mr Whymper is asked by other farmers about conditions on Animal Farm after his visit there. Write down, in play form, or as conversation, the questions he is asked and his replies.

3 In this chapter are things on Animal Farm worse or better than when Jones was master? Give some facts to show why you think as you do.

The trial

Write two newspaper reports about the trial of the four pigs, the three hens, the goose and the sheep. Give each a headline. Write the first report as if it were written by Squealer, showing the pigs in a good light and the animals on trial as evil. Write the second giving the real truth as you see it. What purpose might Napoleon have had in holding the trial?

Chapter 8

Writing

1 By looking at the paragraph headed 'History' at the beginning of this Section decide which of the farmers, Mr Frederick or Mr Pilkington, represents Hitler and which is most like Winston Churchill. Give the evidence that has led you to your decision.

2 As if you were Napoleon, write the victory speech after the battle. Who would you praise the most? Why was your victory so magnificent? Why was the ruin of the windmill unimportant? Whose treacherous hand might have been behind the attack on Animal Farm?

A war map

Draw a map of Animal Farm with house and buildings. Then mark on the map the various stages of the battle that took place there between Frederick and his men and the animals.

Role play

Discuss the plans Frederick and his men might have made after the battle and then act out in character the discussion they might have had about attacking again, making peace or leaving Animal Farm alone.

Chapter 9

Writing

1 Write one of the poems, honouring Napoleon, that were recited during one of the Spontaneous Demonstrations.

2 Some animals did dare to criticise the Napoleon regime. Write the conversation two rebellious hens might have had in secret about it.

3 It might have been Mr Whymper who arranged with the slaughterer to take Boxer away. Write in play form the discussion he had with the slaughterer, Alfred Simmonds.

Chapter 10

The wheel of change

'The creatures outside looked from pig to man and from man to pig, and from pig to man again; but already it was impossible to say which was which.'
Look at the top of page 91. Set this out on a double page of your book and put this at the top of your double page.
Then, using as many squares as you need, pick out and write down in note form the most important changes that have turned 'Animal Farm' back into 'Manor Farm'.

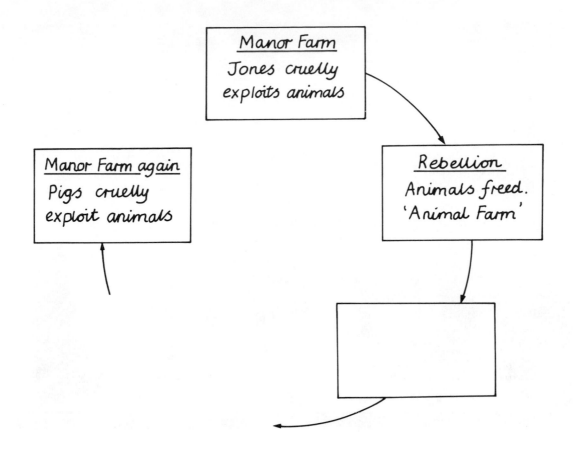

Further study activities

Illustrations

You have been asked to provide four single page pictures to illustrate the book. Pick four incidents that you think would be suitable. Then, either describe what you would put in the illustrations or draw them.

Advertisement

You need a display poster for the book. This might show the cover illustration, which you could design. You would also need a sentence to describe the book. This should tell you why the book is generally interesting.

Cartoons

Look at the cartoons on page 92. Imagine that the first cartoon illustrates the unveiling of a portrait of Napoleon. Write either the poem Minimus has made or the speech Squealer will deliver in honour of the occasion. Whichever you choose, write Napoleon's speech which closes the ceremony.

The second cartoon depicts the paperwork that Squealer explains is a necessary and onerous task for the pigs. Write three examples of the kind of paperwork being produced. It may be anything from a grocery order – which would reflect the pigs' greed and their lack of consideration for the other animals – to the draft of a speech explaining why longer hours are necessary, boasting about record production, insulting Snowball, etc.

Writing

1 Does Mollie have any regrets about working for human beings again? Write, as if you were Mollie, her opinion of the animal revolution, describing some of the things that happened and her attitude to them and saying how she feels now. If you need to refresh your memory about her, looking at Chapters 3, 4 and 5 will help.

2 Write, as if you were Benjamin the donkey, his views of the revolution.

3 Write a short book review of *Animal Farm*, mentioning things you like and dislike about the book and picking out one particular part of it you find most interesting.

4 Which character in the book were you sorriest for? Write an account of what that character did, what happened to it and explain your feelings about it.

Press conference

Napoleon, Squealer and three other pigs are giving a press conference to explain how they have helped the animals on Animal Farm. Three or four journalists are to ask questions. These might be searching questions such as: Why do only the pigs on the farm get the barley? *or* Why is the windmill not used to supply electricity for all the animals on the farm? Choose the parts you will play and then, in character, act out what might happen.

Finding out about the the Russian Revolution

With the help of reference books each member of a group answers one of these questions:

1 When and where did the revolution begin?

2 Who was Lenin and what part did he play in it?

3 Who was Trotsky and what part did he play?

4 When did Lenin die and who took over from him?

5 When was Trotsky driven out of Russia and what happened to him after that?

6 Who was Stalin and what sort of things did he do when he came to power?

7 What trials took place in Russia in 1937–1938 and what happened to those accused?

8 When did Stalin sign a pact of friendship with Hitler and Nazi Germany?

9 When did Hitler invade Russia?

Then, with the help of the information researched, the class discuss the parallels they can see between incidents in *Animal Farm* and incidents in the history of Russia after the revolution.

Does power corrupt?

Orwell's book suggests that those who are given power cannot be trusted to use it for the general good. Is this true only of a totalitarian government like that of Stalinist Russia? Can other forms of government be trusted to use their power wisely and well? Or is it true that most governments, if given power, will try to use it for their own personal ends?

Assessing an answer

The class read the following essays about topics from the book, and then discuss the facts they contain. Are all the facts mentioned and taken from the book correct? Consider the opinions. Are these sensible and well argued. How well is each essay written? Is it clear and easy to follow?

Each essay could then be voted a mark, out of 40, by the class.

Essay One

Title: How does Napoleon gain control of Animal Farm?

The book is called 'Animal Farm' and the author is George Orwell. He also wrote the book '1984'. This book was written in 1945.

It was old major who started it all off by telling the other animals about a dream he had. his dream was that the animals rebelled against humans and that all animals are equal. Later they decided to take over Manor farm and kick out humans. The kicked out humans and changed the farm to 'Animal farm'. To start with their were two leaders Napoleon and Snowball.

Napoleon was a strong fierce looking boar. The only one on the farm. Snowball was more vicious than Napoleon, quicker in speech and more inventive. The animals made 7 commandments which every one had to obey. They were:
1) Whatever goes upon two legs is an enemy.
2) Whatever goes upon four legs is a friend.
3) No animal shall wear clothes.
4) No animal shall sleep in a bed.
5) No animal shall drink alcohol.
6) No animal shall kill any other animal.
7) All animals are equal.

The commandments were soon changed them to suit him self. The cows hadn't been milked for days then when they were milked all the milk and apples disappeared. It was found out the pigs took them because they needed them for their brains.

Napoleon took control by taking a litter of dogs, saying he was going to educate them. He took them and made them obey him – Napoleon took control by expelling Snowball. He lied and said that Snowball was a spy and helping the humans.

Every time some one spoke when they shouldn't the dogs would bark and make them stop talking. When the hens laid eggs Napoleon took the eggs and sold them to buy himself Alcohol.

Snowball drew some plans to build a windmill to make their own electricity. When he was expelled Napoleon said it was his idea and Snowball stole them. Snowball then came back and kicked the windmill down. Napoleon took control by changing the 7 commandments to suit himself.

Napoleon started to sell things to other farmers. He sold some wood to a human and he gave him forged money.

Four pigs confessed that they helped Snowball. They were killed on the spot. They were killed by 4 dogs ripping their throats out. Three hens, a goose and 3 sheep all confessed and were all killed on the spot.

Napoleon started wearing clothes and walking on his back legs. He invited some humans round to play cards. Two people cheated at cards. They all started shouting in anger. The animals outside looked from pig to man and from man to pig. It was impossible to say which was which.

Essay Two

Title: To what extent is 'Animal Farm' more than just a fairy story for children?

'Animal Farm' was written by George Orwell in the 1930's after he had fought against Franco in the spanish civil war. 'Animal Farm' is a small farm run by Mr. Jones. Jones mistreats and rarely feeds his animals. One day Old Major, one of Mr. Jones prize winning pigs, calls a meeting in one of the barns, he says that the animals should revolt as the farm is efficient enough to feed them sufficiently more than what Mr. Jones gives them. After Old Major dies life on the farm becomes worse, and eventually the animals revolt. They chase all the humans out, and the pigs take over as they are the cleverest of all the animals on the farm. The two leaders, Napoleon and Snowball, fall out and Snowball is chased off the farm, with a pack of dogs hard on his heels. The other pig, Napoleon, then takes complete control of the farm. After several skirmishes with humans trying to take over the farm, the pigs rule seems to become just like a dictatorship and life for the other animals on the farm became worse than when Mr. Jones ran the farm. This is the point where the story finishes.

These events are not just a 'fairy story' but an accurate satire on the Russian revolution and on communism right from the taking over of the farm by the animals until after the second attempt to take back the farm by the humans. After this point Orwell concludes that the times on 'Animal Farm' before and some time after the revolution are the same. Old Major represents the ideas of Karl Marx and Lenin. Marx was a german industrialist who started the ideas of communism. It is his ideas on which the system in Russia was based, but the leadership of the ordinary people was supposed to fade away leaving all men equal. This has not happened in Russia, or in any other communist country, and in Orwell's book he concludes that the leadership becomes stronger and stronger and will never fade away as the leaders become more superior to the workers. In 'Animal Farm', after Old Major dies, the animals rebel against Mr. Jones. Mr Jones is based on Tsar Nicholas the second, who was living quite comfortably and ignored the plight of his countrymen who were starving to death. This is what led to the revolution, and the revolution on 'Animal Farm'. Napoleon is based around Joseph Stalin, the leader of the Union of Soviet Socialist Republics. After several years of his rule the Russian people were just as well off as when ruled by Nicholas II, which is contrary to the ideas of communism as food should have been plenty for everyone. Snowball is based on Trotsky. Trotsky was one of the leaders of the Bolshoviks and he trained a seemly useless unexperienced rabble into a well-equipped efficient army of several million men. It was because of Trotsky that the Bolshoviks came to power, he was rewarded with death, assassinated on the orders of Stalin, just as Snowball was after leading the counter attacks against the humans. Before his death Trotsky had made plans for massive industrialisation which Stalin adopted and said that they were his plans called the 'Five Year Plan'. Squealer represents the propaganda. This had a great effect on the Russian people, and it was because of this that Stalin remained a popular figure and remained in power despite the food shortage and that his industrialisation plans were facing failure. The two other farms represent Britain (Pilkington and Foxwood farm) and Germany (Frederick and Pinchfield). Germany was Russia's main enemy as they had a dictator, (even though Stalin was also a dictator really) Adolf Hitler, Germany declared a peace pact with Russia, with which the Russian people were not very pleased (but the propaganda soon changed that) and then Germany turned round and invaded them, catching the Russians off their guard. This invasion of Russia and then of Poland led to the second world war. As in the first world war Russia suffered the greatest number of casualties. After a conflict with America over Cuba, Russia has spent more and more on arms while it's people have suffered more and more. They have suffered as there has not been enough money left to be spent on food and Russia has consequently has had to import food from other countries. This state of affairs did not happen on 'Animal Farm', but their produce was exported to provide luxeries for the pigs while the workers were starving.

Animal farm is based on these facts. These facts are modelled around a small farm in England. Karl Marx's teaching are summed up in this speech by Old Major.

'Whatever goes upon four legs, or has wings, is a friend. And remember also that in fighting against Man, we must not come to resemble him. Even when you have conquered him, do not attempt his vices. No animal must ever sleep in a house, or sleep in a bed, or touch money; or engage in trade. All the habits of Man are evil. And, above all, no animal must ever tyrannize over his own kind. Weak or strong, clever or simple, we are all brothers. No animal must ever kill any other animal. All animals are equal.'

These teachings by Old Major are all significant as they are all broken by the pigs the rulers. In fact the pigs eventually walk on two legs and
'The creatures outside looked from Pig to Man, and from Man to Pig again; but already it was impossible to say which was which.'

The leader, Napoleon, brewed his own beer, slept in a bed, and traded with the other farms through Mr. Whymper, a solicitor. Napoleon sold four hundred eggs, the money which was used to buy grain as the pigs took up all the habits of men, and animals did kill each. These killings happened soon after Napolean took over and after the dogs had chased Snowball off the farm. These incidents compare to the killing of some ten million Russians during Stalin's 'Reign'. People were killed for 'putting nails in butter' and other crimes. On 'Animal Farm' four pigs had their throats torn out for being in contact with Snowball. Three hens were slaughtered for the rebellion over the eggs, a goose was killed for 'having secreted six ears of corn' and eaten them at night, and lastly a sheep was executed for 'having urinated in the drinking pool' urged to do this, supposedly, by Snowball. Although trivial matters, this type of punishment did and does happen in communist Russia. They were called crimes against the state. Stalin was still worshipped and praised by the Russians, even though he has sentenced people to death, because the propaganda was so convincing. This is why no-one dared to opposed Napolean because he was feared, because of his dogs (based on the KGB and other secret police movements). The propaganda was a more democratic way of gaining support for Napoleon, and this was another factor in his unopposed leadership. The part of Old Major's speech which states that 'all animals are equal' is as humans are in Russia, is never found to be true. This statement is changed later by the pigs to 'all animals are equal but some are more equal than others'. As for the rule that no animal shall adopt Man's vices, which the commandment 'No animal shall drink alcohol' was derived was changed to 'no animal shall drink alcohol to excess' after Napoleon became drunk. This shows that the fundamental ideas of 'Animalism' were disappearing as are the fundamental ideas of 'communism' are fading away in Russia.

At the end of 'Animal Farm' the relationship with the Russia revolution ends. Orwell predicts what will happen to life under communism. He predicts that contrary to the ideas of Marx and Lenin, the temporary dictatorship by the proletariat does not slowly fade away, but consolidates and becomes immune from any force trying to undermine its power and it therefore has the lives of everyone at its hands. If their orders are disobeyed they are killed. This is even worse than when Tsar Nicholas was in power. In fact on Animal Farm, Pilkington

> 'Once again congratulated the pigs on the low rations, the long working hours, and the general absence of pampering which he had observed on Animal Farm.'

This shows that the pigs gave the other animals less feed than Jones had. In fact it seems, from the way that Orwell has written this book that communism is just another way of making people work harder for less food and money. I think this is what Orwell is trying to point out in his story, that the animals are being exploited.

To conclude on the answer to why 'Animal Farm' is more than just a fairy story for children 'Animal Farm' is a very accurate and convincing satire on the Russian Revolution and communist ideas. The story tells, in a simple story, the birth of communism, through the revolution, two wars, the failure of industrialisation through to the complete dictatorship of the animals. The story is sometimes sad as it shows the miserable lives of the animals, and it is a very good introduction to anyone wishing to learn about communism as the book has all the facts concisely around a fictional story, simply constructed, around a small farm.

Writing

1 Does the book have a hero or a heroine or is there one character that is more attractive than any of the others? If so, describe the character, saying what he or she does in the book and explaining why you find him or her attractive.

2 Are all the pigs in the book equally villainous? Write about three of them, describing what they do and showing that some of them are more villainous than others.

3 Describe two or three incidents in the book that you found amusing and show how Orwell has used humour to show up some of the foolishness of those characters involved and human beings generally.

Animal Farm as a play

Here is the opening scene of a play version of *Animal Farm*. Act it out in groups. If you can, make a simple tune for the songs.

How does the author overcome the problem of a story-teller? What, from this sample, do you think has been gained or lost by turning the book into a play?

Choose any scene you wish and turn it into play form using either your own method or the one shown in the sample.

Act one

A Boy's bedroom. A large bookcase. A toy chest on it, a child's brightly coloured farm set.

A Boy some eight or nine years old strolls forward. He stands on a chair and selects a book from the top of the bookcase. He moves down stage and sits on the toy box.

Boy   (*reading*) Animal Farm. A fairy story by George Orwell.

The Boy's room disappears. The farmhouse, and the farm gate take over the stage. Mr Jones is revealed standing by the gate. On the gate is painted a slogan: 'Manor Farm'.

'In the past Mr Jones, although a cruel master, had been a capable farmer. But now he spent more and more time in the Red Lion. Every night he came home drunk.

Mr Jones   (*singing*) **Who made the cows and sheep so meek?**
Who feeds the cats and dogs their meat?
Who's the loving father
Of fur and feather?
Man, bounteous man! Wonderful man!

Boy   His farm was now thoroughly neglected. The fields were full of weeds and the animals were underfed and in poor condition.

Mr Jones   **Who guards his servants with a gun**
And, when their time to leave has come,
Who leads pigs and horses
To slaughter houses?
Man, masterful man. Powerful man.

Boy   He went up the stairs, undressed and climbed unsteadily into bed.

Throughout the play what the Boy describes happens around him. The black figures set elements of the farm, become animals, execute mimes, or speak scenes of dialogue.
Jones makes his way to the door of his house, kicks off his boots, and, still singing, goes up the stairs. Finally, the bedroom light goes out.

Boy As soon as the light was out, there was a stirring and a fluttering throughout the farm. Word had gone round the animals that there was to be a secret meeting in the big barn. Old Major, the stud boar had something to say . . . .

Lights up on the barn full of animals. Old Major, a large old pig, centre stage. Hens, Pigeons, Sheep, Cows; Boxer, a huge cart horse; Clover, a stout motherly mare; Muriel, the white goat; Benjamin, the old donkey.

Major Last night I had a strange dream. Many years ago when I was a little pig, my mother and the other sows used to sing a secret and ancient song. I learnt that song. I learnt its words, I learnt its music. But it has long since passed out of my mind. Last night it came back to me. In my dream . . . .

(*He sings.*) **Beasts of England! Beasts of Ireland!**
Beasts of land and sea and skies!
Hear the hoofbeats of tomorrow!
See the golden future rise!

The animals stir, but he quietens them.

Wait – no noise – wait! Or we'll wake up Jones! I am over twelve years old and have had over four hundred children. I think I understand the nature of life on this earth as well as any animal now living. Listen carefully, for I do not think that I shall be with you for many months longer.

Mollie, a foolish pretty white mare, rushes in late.

Clover Why are you late, Mollie?
Mollie Sorry . . . I had a stone in my hoof. (*She shrugs girlishly.*)
Major Listen!

(*He sings*) **How does the life of an animal pass?**
In endless drudgery.
What's the first lesson an animal learns?
To endure its slavery.
How does the life of an animal end?
In cruel butchery.

Is this simply part of the order of nature? No, Comrades. This farm would support a dozen horses, twenty cows, hundreds of sheep – all of them living in comfort and dignity beyond our imagining. Our labour tills the soil, our dung fertilises it. And yet there is not one of us who owns more than his bare skin. The produce of our labour is stolen from us by human beings. Man is our only enemy.

He's the lord of all the animals
Yet he can't lay eggs or pull a plough.
He's the greatest of all criminals,
Stealing wool from the sheep and milk from the cow.
He's the lord of all the animals
And the only one who's no use.
For he consumes, consumes, consumes,
But he cannot produce.

Never listen when they tell you that man and the animals have a common interest – that the prosperity of the one is the prosperity of the other. You cows: what has happened to the milk which should feed you calves?

The Cows	It has gone down the throat of our enemy! Man!
Major	And you hens: what has happened to the eggs you have laid?
The Hens	They have been stolen from us by our enemy! Man!
Major	And you, Clover: where are your six children, the foals who should have been the support and pleasure of your old age?
Clover	They were sold at a year old by our enemy, man! I will never see them again.
Major	But even the miserable lives that we lead are not allowed to reach their natural span. You young pigs will scream your lives out on the block within a year – every one of you.
Young Pigs	(*in terror*): No! No! No!

Major	Yes! To that horror we must all come. Cows, pigs, hens, sheep, everyone – even you Boxer. They'll butcher you.
Boxer	Why me? I work hard for them.
Major	The day that those great muscles of yours lose their power, Jones will sell you to the knacker, who will cut your throat and boil you down for dog food. What must we do? Why, work, comrades. Work night and day, body and soul, for the overthrow of the human race! Rebellion! That is my message to you, comrades! Rebellion! I do not know when the rebellion will come, but I know as surely as I see the straw beneath my feet that sooner or later justice will be done. But when you conquer man do not adopt his vices. Remember that all animals are equal!
Snowball	Old Major, what about the wild creatures – the rats and the rabbits – are they our friends or our enemies?
Major	You must decide. You must learn to vote. Each one of you must have a say in the way we lead our lives. I propose this question to the meeting: Are the wild creatures comrades? All those in favour . . .

They begin to take a vote by raising their trotters and hooves. As the Boy speaks the action freezes.

Boy	And so the animals learnt to vote for the first time. It was agreed by an overwhelming majority that the wild creatures were comrades.
All the Animals	Agreed, agreed!
Boy	There was only one vote against: the cat. She was afterwards discovered to have voted on both sides.
Major and all the animals	**Beasts of England! Beasts of Ireland! Beasts of land and sea and skies! Hear the hoofbeats of tomorrow! See the golden future rise!**
	Now the day of beasts is coming, Tyrant man shall lose his throne And the shining fields of England Shall be trod by beasts alone.

Pull the rings from out of your noses!
Tear the saddle from your back!
Bit and spur shall rust forever,
Cruel whips no more shall crack.

Beasts of England, seize the prizes,
Wheat and barley, oats and hay,
Clover, beans and mangel wurzels
Shall be ours upon that day,
Shall be ours upon that –

Mr Jones flings open his bedroom window

Mr Jones   *(shouting)* QU-I-ET!

The Animals freeze, holding their breath.

What's bothering you? Is it a fox? A fox, is it?

He reaches for his shotgun and fires into the darkness. The lights fade as the meeting of the Animals breaks up quickly and silently.

Boy   Three nights later, Old Major died peacefully in his sleep.

The Animals watch as Old Major slowly leaves.

His body was buried at the foot of the orchard.

from *Animal Farm* (the play) adapted by Peter Hall

Wider reading

You should not limit your wider reading to fiction. A real help to your understanding of *Animal Farm* would be material from:

The Downfall of Tzarist Russia – Elizabeth Roberts (Methuen);
Russian Revolution 1900–1930 (Deutsch).

George Orwell's *1984* is an even grimmer warning against tyranny than *Animal Farm*.
Pages 105–219 of *1985* by Antony Burgess foresees a different kind of horror, as does *Brave New World* by Aldous Huxley.

7

Poetry Project

Think about poetry

This section encourages you to think about, understand and write poetry. Young people today are much more likely to enjoy and write poetry than their parents and grandparents. But many people of all ages are still frightened of poetry. Read this poem by Wendy Cope. The idea of the poem comes from the piece she has read in a newspaper, printed at the top.

At the moment, if you're seen reading poetry in a train,
the carriage empties instantly.

Andrew Motion in a *Guardian* interview

Indeed 'tis true. I travel here and there
On British Rail a lot. I've often said
That if you haven't got the first-class fare
You really need a book of verse instead.
Then, should you find that all the seats are taken,
Brandish your Edward Thomas, Yeats or Pound.
Your fellow-passengers, severely shaken,
Will almost all be loath to stick around.
Recent research in railway sociology
Shows it's best to read the stuff aloud:
A few choice bits from Motion's new anthology
And you'll be lonelier than any cloud.
This stratagem's a godsend to recluses
And demonstrates that poetry has its uses.

Discussion

Discuss the poem in small groups, considering these questions. Is the poem serious? Could you really empty a railway carriage by reading poetry aloud? Could you embarrass people with poetry? What are your feelings about poetry, compared to plays, or maths or geography for instance? Do you have a special feeling about poetry? Do you think poetry is about particular types of things? Does poetry need to rhyme? How do you recognise a poem from a piece of prose?
Which of the two pieces on page 107, for instance, is a poem? How do you know?

The Rebel

When I die I'm sure I will have a big funeral, curiosity seekers coming to see
if I am really dead or just trying to make trouble.

The Rebel

When I
die
I'm sure
I will have a
Big Funeral . . .
Curiosity
seekers . . .
coming to see
if I
am really
Dead . . .
or just
trying to make
Trouble . . .

Mari Evans

Discussion

Why did Mari Evans decide to put her thought
in the poetry form? What advantages has she
gained? Consider which words she's
emphasised, and how. What use has she made
of pauses?

The purpose of poetry

The aim of any writer is to tell the reader something – an idea, a feeling or simply some information. He or she may want to make the reader sympathise, or annoy the reader, or make him laugh; he may wish to make the reader re-think, look at something from a different angle; he may simply want to tell him something, explain an idea or a process; he may even want to deceive, trick the reader into thinking or doing something.

Poetry is simply one method of saying something. It can be more dramatic than prose, enabling the writer to use rhyme and rhythm or to emphasise certain words by their placing in the poem; poetry can also emphasise more easily by such devices as repetition or the use of contrasting short and long lines – look at how Mari Evans has emphasised the important words in her poem.

Once we have grasped that poetry is simply a form of saying something, attitudes such as the one Wendy Cope jokingly exploits in her poem disappear.

How to approach the poetry project

There are eight poems for you to consider. In groups of five or six consider them in the order they appear. One member of the group should read the poem aloud to the others; it is best if you each have a copy of the poem, so that you can write your first thoughts on the sheet. After the first reading take a little time to consider the poem again before everyone makes a statement or asks a question about it. As a group, you are considering such things as: What is the purpose of the poem? What is the author trying to say to us? What interests you about the shape of his or her poem? What particular words or phrases interest you? Is the rhythm of the poem fast or slow? Does it vary? Do the lines run on without a break, or do they end with a punctuation mark? Are there any repeated patterns of words or rhythm in the poem? Are there any interesting similes or metaphors? Does the above help the writer to say what he or she intends more clearly? Do you agree or sympathise with what is being said?

After you have all made a statement about the poem, choose somebody (a different person for each poem) to tell the rest of the class what the group's feelings are.

After two group and general discussions, everybody should choose one of the poems and write a piece about it for his or her folder. The piece should explain what the poet is saying and have some comments on the way it is said. Use some quotations from the poem to back up your statements.

For two of the poems, try to use the method and patterns of the poem to write a similar one of your own, as is illustrated on pages 113 and 114.

The poetry project should take about three weeks. At the end you will have a Poetry Journal with essays on four poems and two poems of your own.

1 – Hugger Mugger

I'd sooner be
Jumped and thumped and dumped
I'd sooner be
Slugged and mugged . . . than bugged
And clobbered with a slobbering
Kiss by my Auntie Jean:

You know what I mean:

Whenever she comes to stay,
You know you're bound
To get one
A quick
short
peck
would
be
O.K.
But this is a
Whacking great
Smacking great
Wet one!
All whoosh and spit
And crunch and squeeze
And 'Dear little boy!'
And 'Auntie's missed you!'
And 'Come to Auntie, she
Hasn't kissed you!'
Please don't do it Auntie,
PLEASE
Or if you've absolutely
Got to
And nothing on earth can persuade you
Not to
The trick
Is to make it
Quick
You know what I mean?
For as things are
I really would far
Far sooner be
Jumped and thumped . . . than hugged
And clobbered with a slobbering
Kiss by my Auntie
Jean!   Kit Wright

Help!

For the first few poems you will be given a few
pieces of advice that might help you start your
discussion.
Look, in this poem, for different patterns of
words, for strong verbs and adjectives. What
use is made of them? How has the author
made the poem dramatic?

Your own version

Perhaps you have an uncle or acquaintance
who insists on slapping you on the back and
bellowing, 'How goes it?' Any persistent,
annoying habit will be a good subject,
especially if it's not meant to be annoying. You
needn't limit it to your family. Look at this
beginning, for instance:

I'd sooner have
Awful, Lousy, Rotten
I'd sooner have
'Get in detention' written
On my book than a
single
feeble
TICK.

2 – Palm Tree King

Because I come from the West Indies
certain people in England seem to think
I is a expert on palm trees

So not wanting to sever dis link
with me native roots (know what ah mean?)
or to disappoint dese culture vulture
I does smile cool as seabreeze

and say to dem
which specimen
you interested in
cause you talking
to the right man
I is palm tree king
I know palm tree history
like de palm o me hand
In fact me navel string
bury under a palm tree

If you think de queen could wave
you ain't seen nothing yet
till you see the Roystonea regia
– that is the royal palm –
with she crown of leaves
waving calm-calm
over the blue Caribbean carpet
nearly 100 feet of royal highness

But let we get down to business
Tell me what you want to know
How tall a palm tree does grow?
What is the biggest coconut I ever see?
What is the average length of the leaf?

Don't expect me to be brief
cause palm tree history
is a long-long story
Anyway why you so interested
in length and circumference?
That kind of talk so ordinary
That don't touch the essence
of palm tree mystery
That is no challenge
to a palm tree historian like me

If you insist on statistics
why don't you pose a question
with some mathematical profundity?

Ask me something more tricky
like if an American tourist with a camera
takes nine minutes to climb a coconut tree
how long a English tourist without a camera
would take to climb the same coconut tree?

That is a problem pardner
Now ah coming coming harder

If 6 straw hat
and half a dozen bikini
multiply by the same number of coconut tree
equal one postcard
how many miles of straw hat
you need to make a tourist industry?

That is problem pardner
Find the solution
and you got a revolution

But before you say anything
let I palm tree king
give you dis warning
Ah want the answer in metric
it kind of rhyme with tropic
Because it sounds more exotic.

John Agard

Help!

Ask a silly question and I'll give you the silly answer
you deserve.
What kind of prejudice is at the centre of the poem?
How serious is the author?

Imitation

If you try with this poem, notice how the accent
helps. One type of imitation might start:

Cos I cum from a village
Reet art int sticks
Rather superior people seem to imagine I know
All abaht 'ens an' eggs,

3 – Reading Scheme

Here is Peter. Here is Jane. They like fun.
Jane has a big doll. Peter has a ball.
Look, Jane, look! Look at the dog! See him run!

Here is Mummy. She has baked a bun.
Here is the milkman. He has come to call.
Here is Peter. Here is Jane; They like fun.

Go Peter! Go Jane! Come, milkman, come!
The milkman likes Mummy. She likes them all.
Look, Jane, look! Look at the dog! See him run!

Here are the curtains. They shut out the sun.
Let us peep! On tiptoe Jane! You are small!
Here is Peter. Here is Jane. They like fun.

I hear a car, Jane. The milkman looks glum.
Here is Daddy in his car. Daddy is tall.
Look, Jane, look! Look at the dog! See him run!

Daddy looks very cross. Has he a gun?
Up milkman! Up milkman! Over the wall!
Here is Peter. Here is Jane. They like fun.
Look Jane, look! Look at the dog! See him run!

Wendy Cope

Help!

Notice how carefully the writer follows the
child's reading scheme, the words repeated
many times in different structures.
If you try imitation, don't overdo it. Keep it
sounding innocent – and clean! Of course any
adult dispute will be acceptable matter – Daddy
or Mummy late home, for instance.

Read this poem and then try to write one that uses the same method to make a point about human beings. Choose another animal – sheep, pig or parrot, for example. The animal you choose will decide the type of part you are playing. Try to imitate the shape of 'Warty Bliggens'.

Before you begin look at the attempt on page 114 called 'Cybil Shepherd' by someone of your own age. How well has she captured the idea of the original poem?

4 – warty bliggens the toad

i met a toad
the other day by the name
of warty bliggens
he was sitting under
a toadstool
feeling contented
he explained that when the cosmos
was created
that toadstool was especially
planned for his personal
shelter from sun and rain
thought out and prepared
for him

do not tell me
said warty bliggens
that there is not a purpose
in the universe
the thought is blasphemy
a little more
conversation revealed
that warty bliggens
considers himself to be

the centre of the said
universe
the earth exists
to grow toadstools for him
to sit under
the sun to give him light
by day and the moon
and wheeling constellations
to make beautiful
the night for the sake of
warty bliggens

to what act of yours
do you impute
this interest on the part
of the creator
of the universe
i asked him
why is it that you
are so greatly favoured

ask rather
said warty bliggens
what the universe
has done to deserve me
if i were a
human being i would
not laugh
too complacently
at poor warty bliggens
for similar
absurdities
have only too often
lodged in the crinkles
of the human cerebrum

113

Cybil Shepherd the sheep

I met a sheep the other day
by the name of Cybil Shepherd
He was standing in a field
of Clover.
Waiting for someone to follow
I asked him
'Why do you spend all your life
eating, sleeping and following other sheep
around in ever-widening circles.'

He explained to me
When the universe
was created
Other sheep were created especially for mine
personal use
I then can follow the other sheep
and
don't have to think for myself.
I do as they do
and I don't have a care in the whole universe.

To what act of yours do you impute
this interest on the part of the creater
of the said universe.
I asked him
'why is it
you are so greatly loved.'

Ask rather said
Cybil Shepherd
What has this universe
done to deserve me.
If I were a human being
I would not talk about Cybil shepherd
like this
nor would I laugh complacently
at poor old Cybil

For there are similar people
on this universe
who follow others around
in ever winding circles
who do as what someone else says
and
who never thinks for himself.

5 – Emily writes such a good letter

Mabel was married last week
So now only Tom left

The doctor didn't like Arthur's cough
I have been in bed since Easter

A touch of the old trouble

I am downstairs today
As I write this
I can hear Arthur roaming overhead

He loves to roam
Thank heavens he has plenty of space to roam in

We have seven bedrooms
And an annexe

Which leaves a flat for the chauffeur and his wife

We have much to be thankful for

The new vicar came yesterday
People say he brings a breath of fresh air

He leaves me cold
I do not think he is a gentleman

Yes, I remember Maurice very well
Fancy getting married at his age
She must be a fool

You knew May had moved?
Since Edward died she has been much alone

It was cancer

No, I know nothing of Maud
I never wish to hear her name again
In my opinion Maud
Is an evil woman

Our char has left
And good riddance too
Wages are very high in Tonbridge

Write and tell me how you are, dear,
And the girls,
Phoebe and Rose
They must be a great comfort to you
Phoebe and Rose.

Stevie Smith

Help!

If you try to imitate this poem, a good starting point would be to listen to one end of a telephone conversation. Simply writing down what is said would make a poem in itself.

6 – False Security

I remember the dread with which I at a quarter past four
Let go with a bang behind me our house front door
And, clutching a present for my dear little hostess tight,
Sailed out for the children's party into the night
Or rather the gathering night. For still some boys
In the near municipal acres were making a noise
Shuffling in fallen leaves and shouting and whistling
And running past hedges of hawthorn, spikey and bristling.
And black in the oncoming darkness stood out the trees
And pink shone the ponds in the sunset ready to freeze
And all was still and ominous waiting for dark
And the keeper was ringing his closing bell in the park
And the arc lights started to fizzle and burst into mauve
As I climbed West Hill to the great big house in The Grove,
Where the children's party was and the dear little hostess.
But halfway up stood the empty house where the ghost is.
I crossed to the other side and under the arc
Made a rush for the next kind lamp-post out of the dark
And so to the next and the next till I reached the top
Where the grove branched off to the left. Then ready to drop
I ran to the ironwork gateway of number seven
Secure at last on the lamplit fringe of Heaven.
Oh who can say how subtle and safe one feels
Shod in one's children's sandals from Daniel Neal's,
Clad in one's party clothes made of stuff from Heal's?
And who can still one's thrill at the candle shine
On cakes and ices and jelly and blackcurrant wine,
And the warm little feel of my hostess's hand in mine?
Can I forget my delight at the conjuring show?
And wasn't I proud that I was the last to go?
Too overexcited and pleased with myself to know
That the words I heard my hostess's mother employ
To a guest departing, would ever diminish my joy,
I WONDER WHERE JULIA FOUND THAT STRANGE,
RATHER COMMON LITTLE BOY?

John Betjeman

7 – Wires

The widest prairies have electric fences,
For though old cattle know they must not stray
Young steers are always scenting purer water
Not here but anywhere. Beyond the wires

Leads them to blunder up against the wires
Whose muscle-shredding violence gives no quarter.
Young steers become old cattle from that day,
Electric limits to their widest senses.

Philip Larkin

Help!

This means more than it says. How can you
relate the cattle to human beings?

8 – Mountain Lion

Climbing through the January snow, into the Lobo Canyon
Dark grow the spruce-trees, blue is the balsam, water sounds,
    still unfrozen, and the trail is still evident.
Men!
Two men!
Men! The only animal in the world to fear!

They hesitate.
We hesitate.
They have a gun.
We have no gun.

Then we all advance, to meet.

Two Mexicans, strangers, emerging out of the dark and snow and
    inwardness of the Lobo Valley.
What are they doing here on this vanishing trail?

What is he carrying?
Something yellow.
A deer?

Qué tiene, amigo?
León –

He smiles, foolishly, as if he were caught doing wrong.
And we smile, foolishly, as if we didn't know.
He is quite gentle and dark-faced.

117

It is a mountain lion,
A long, long slim cat, yellow like a lioness.
Dead.

He trapped her this morning, he says, smiling foolishly.

Lift up her face,
Her round, bright face, bright as frost.
Her round, fine-fashioned head, with two dead ears;
And stripes in the brilliant frost of her face, sharp, fine dark rays
Dark, keen, fine rays in the brilliant frost of her face.
Beautiful dead eyes.

Hermoso es!

They go out towards the open;
We go on into the gloom of Lobo.
And above the trees I found her lair,
A hole in the blood-orange brilliant rocks that stick up, a little cave.
And bones, and twigs, and a perilous ascent.

So, she will never leap up that way again, with the yellow flash of a mountain
     lion's long shoot!
And her bright striped frost-face will never watch any more, out of the shadow
     of the cave in the blood-orange rock,
Above the trees of the Lobo dark valley-mouth!

Instead, I look out.
And out to the dim of the desert, like a dream, never real;
To the snow of the Sangre de Cristo mountains, the ice of the mountains of
     Picoris,
And near across at the opposite step of snow, green trees motionless
     standing in snow, like a Christmas toy.

And I think in this empty world there was room for me and a mountain lion.
And I think in the world beyond, how easily we might spare a million or two of
     humans
And never miss them.
Yet what a gap in the world, the missing white frost-face of that slim yellow
     mountain lion!

D. H. Lawrence

8

Spring and Port Wine

Bill Naughton

The looming presence of Rafe

What are your neighbours like? Are you sure? If you could see into their house what would they be doing? How would they be getting on with each other?

In plays about the family like *Spring and Port Wine* we, the audience, are privileged neighbours. We can see through the walls into the Crompton family. We see a series of dramatic events over one weekend. The children are all grown-up; they have their own little quarrels with each other. But over the family looms the presence of Rafe, the father.

When we first see into the Crompton family Rafe is not there – in person. But in spirit he is. Rafe dominates the household even when he isn't there.

Quotations

Rafe does not appear until a third of the way through Act One. The author builds up our expectation of him by what the rest of the family say.

Find each of these quotations. They are in chronological order. (the order in which they appear in the script). For each one write down:

1 Who said it?
2 What is being referred to?
3 What do the words show about the speaker's feelings towards Rafe?

'You know he likes everything to be just so.'

'God help you if he ever finds out.'

'Rafe always likes to come home to everything spick and span on a Friday.'

'Better get the Airwick spray out, mate.'

'Be careful your dad doesn't hear you.'

'First come, first served. Come on – who's game?'

Role play – in pairs

One person chooses the role of a family member other than Rafe. The other is a friend who has been brought home to tea. He, or she, has listened to the conversation before Rafe appears. Anxiously, the friend questions the member of the family:

'What's your Dad really like?'
'Why are you all so scared of him?'

The member of the family will relate a few incidents to illustrate, his or her, point of view – make them up. Remember attitudes vary. Daisy is very loyal; Harold likes to think he can rebel.

Swop roles and then write up your interview.

A diagram

Rafe appears and with his first remark shows the truth of what his family has said about him. The play now revolves around Rafe – and the herring. Copy the diagram on page 121 and write in the boxes what you think each of the characters feels about Rafe at the end of Act One.

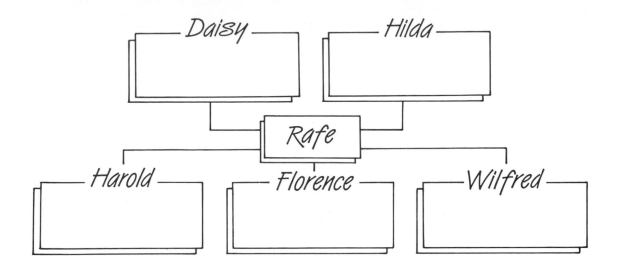

Rafe at the end of the play

It is not unusual for a play to centre on one character; but usually that character changes, the events of the play affect him or her.

Discussion

Is Rafe a changed man at the end of the play,
or have we simply found out more about him?
Read this review of the play's ending:

> 'How will the old tyrant react, when his life's ambitions come tumbling down?'
> Alas, Bill Naughton who has it in him to solve that problem as brilliantly as he has set it up and allowed it to develop, shirks that task altogether. In the closing twenty minutes of the play he lets it go to pieces simply making old Rafe Crompton undergo the most incredible change of heart. From one moment to the next he turns into a dear old soul who understands everyone and everything (even the fact that his wife tried to pick a lock of his money box and, when this failed, pawned his brand-new overcoat) . . . Naughton . . . suddenly turns himself into a sloppy writer for one of the cheaper women's magazines . . .
>
> Martin Esslin, *Plays and Players*

Is there any truth in what this critic says? Consider, in particular, the phrase *'incredible* change of heart'.

Rafe's diary

Write the diary of Rafe, recording his feelings about the main events in the play. You will have to make your judgement about the real character of Rafe before you begin.
For instance, he might show more understanding of Hilda than his behaviour seems to suggest. He might be extremely upset that he is having to do what he feels is for her own good, and is even planning to relent and repent when he thinks it right to do so. On the other hand you might show him to be outraged and disgusted, until he suddenly sees the error of his ways.

Other relationships

As well as the characters revolving round Rafe they also react to each other.

Role play

Play out these imaginary scenes in the family:

1 *Daisy – Hilda*
Daisy discusses with Hilda if there is any other reason why she is off herrings. She could hint at pregnancy, for instance. How would Hilda react?

2 *Daisy – Wilfred*
Wilfred is in bed after his faint. Daisy talks to him about the herring and the cat. She talks about her relationship with Rafe and asks Wilfred not to leave home as he is her youngest son.

3 *Florence – Hilda*
Florence advises Hilda about leaving home. She could be all for it or she could suggest the problems Hilda would find at her age.

Outside the family, characters like Betsy and Arthur have an important influence on the plot. Act out the following scenes.

4 *Daisy – Betsy*
Betsy asks next day (Tuesday) what has happened. How much does Daisy tell her? Does she resume a friendship?

5 *Betsy and an imaginary neighbour*
Betsy spreads the news about what has been going on to a gossip in the street. 'Have you heard, etc . . .?'

6 *Florence – Arthur*
They discuss whether they could ever have Rafe to live with them, if Daisy died first.

Study the photographs

Study these photographs of the actors for a production of the play. Assign the actors by their roles and give reasons for your choice.

Atmosphere in plays

The atmosphere is very important to the play. The author wants to set just the right atmosphere to help you believe in his or her play. For two hours or so you have to suspend your belief in the real world and believe only in the play. This can be helped by the setting.

What is the set like?

Read the description of the set at the beginning of Act One. How would you make it look like a prosperous, working-class home in 1965? What touches would you add to those already described? What could you research into to find out how a home looked in 1965? We know they have television, but what wouldn't they have? Make a sketch or sketches of the set.

The atmosphere created by the characters

The atmosphere the author wants in the first act is one of claustrophobia for the young people. They are all bursting with the desire to break out of the home and their father's tyranny. As young people yourselves you are meant to feel for them. But there are also hints that they are comfortable in their home and do not really want, or have not the courage, to leave the nest. Note how Florence behaves, for instance, when Arthur proposes immediate marriage. This opens up the dramatic possibilities of the play and makes it more interesting than if they were just hell-bent on getting out.

Quotations

Using quotes from the play show what effect Daisy has on the atmosphere of the home.
Using quotes from the play show how the younger members of the family feel hemmed in.
Using quotes from the play show how the atmosphere changes in the last scene.

The issues

The play is about:
the role of the father in a family;
the role of the mother in a family;
democracy within a family unit;
family finance – how a family spends its income;
the desire of young people to leave home and their desire for freedom to live their own lives;
the generation gap;
the desire of parents to protect their children from outside influences.

Discussion

In small groups discuss what the author is
trying to teach us about families in this play.
Where do you think his sympathies lie?

The world outside the play

As well as the world of the play as portrayed on the stage a good author makes us believe in a world outside it. We are asked to imagine that the characters work, for instance. The author also deliberately contrasts the home of Betsy Jane and her husband and that of the Cromptons.
Also, outside the world of the play on the stage, we are asked to believe that important dramatic events took place.

Quotations

1 Using quotations, show how we know that
  Florence, Hilda, Wilfred, Harold, Arthur
  and Rafe have jobs.

2 Using quotations, show the difference
  between Betsy Jane's home and the
  Cromptons'.

Writing

1 Write, as a play, the conversation that Arthur and Florence have about their marriage as they walk on the moors behind Rafe.

2 Write, again as a play, the conversation Hilda has with Betsy Jane about leaving home and going to London.

Life after the play

A good play leaves us thinking about the end. If the play has convinced us, we will wonder what will happen after the fall of the stage curtain. Read again the piece on page 121 about Rafe at the end of the play.
Write down how satisfactory you found the end of the play. Is the change in Rafe too great, or is he just behaving in a different way to achieve his own ends? Will Wilfred and Harold leave home immediately or decide to stay? Will Hilda eventually go to London? What kind of marriage will Florence and Arthur have? What will the relationship of Rafe and Daisy be like now? Will Betsy Jane try to resume her friendship with Daisy? You could write it as a story called 'Summer and . . .' (complete the title).

Dramatic surprises

A good play can be full of dramatic surprises. It is one of the skills of the dramatist to provide them.

In this play there is the gradual build-up of the character of Rafe as a tyrant and a dictator. When Daisy opens the cabinet and pawns the overcoat, or is aided and abetted by Betsy Jane to do so, we expect a great explosion of anger from Rafe. After how he reacted to the herring, how will he react to this much larger issue? We are on tenterhooks waiting for it. Yet, when he discovers what Daisy has done, he behaves in a most tender way. This is a dramatic surprise.

Discuss in small groups

What other surprises are there in the play?

Write about the photographs

Below and on page 128 there are three dramatic moments from *Spring and Port Wine*. Write a short paragraph explaining what you think is happening in each picture and say how successfully the moments have been captured by the facial expressions, posture and placing of the characters.

Further study activities

Quotations

1 There is a great deal of talk about money in the play. Using quotes show how it has affected the characters' lives, particularly Betsy Jane, and Daisy and Rafe in their early years of marriage.

2 Rafe's character is based on the past. He can't really cope with the present. Use quotations to prove this.

Discussion

1 'You talk about not telling him a lie – why, all your life is a flaming lie, if you ask me. How can a man run a home? That's a woman's job, always has been. A man has no right to attempt it. It's not natural.'

How justified is this criticism by Betsy Jane? Is the play mainly about how some women are treated?

2 Show how Florence supports her father in Act One. Show how she is a bit like him. Does a great change come over her?

3 Show how, by what they do and say, the two outside characters – Betsy Jane and Arthur – are important to the plot of the play.

4 'Rafe is very unfair to his children. He is trying to mould them like himself. His house is a happy place when he is not there.' Agree or disagree using quotations.

Writing

1 Hilda writes a letter to Vy Hopkins asking about jobs in London. She tells her about what has happened and her relationship with her father.

2 Write about Daisy's role in the home. Is she happy with it? Does she need to depend on Rafe so much?

3 If you have studied *Hobson's Choice*, write about how conflict is an essential ingredient in both plays.

4 Write part of a new scene in which Rafe exploded when he learnt about the money-box and coat. What might be the reaction of Daisy and the rest of the family?

Wider reading – a play project

Family relationships

Spring and Port Wine and the two plays dealt with in the following sections, *Hobson's Choice* and *An Inspector Calls*, have enough in common for them to form the basis of a play project in which you could compare plot, characters and the writers' purposes. Each play is based on family relationships; in each case the father exerts a powerful influence on his family; in each case that influence is either lost or diminished by the events of the play – there is rebellion by the children against their fathers' perception of the family, the world outside and the relationship between children and parents. Of course the agents of the disturbance and eventual change within the families are vastly different – an uneaten kipper, a mysterious Inspector and a daughter who wants to marry beneath her. Nevertheless, the purposes of the authors are sufficiently similar for you to form relevant comparisons. Each author favours the change in the established order that his play shows. Compare, for instance, the way Hobson and Birling see their positions in society – although *An Inspector Calls* was written in 1946, it is set in 1912, only three years before the first production of *Hobson's Choice*. Birling, unlike Hobson and Rafe, fails to learn the lesson of the play's action, but the lesson is clear enough, and his children learn from it.

Each play shows family relationships very differently from the majority of plays being written today. If you study *Billy Liar* by Keith Waterhouse as a fourth play in your project, you will immediately see a striking difference. The first night audiences of *Hobson's Choice* and *An Inspector Calls* would have been shocked not only by the language, but by the presentation of the father (Geoffrey), the sarcastic open rebellion of Billy, his lack of respect not only for his father and mother, but for his aged grandmother, presented as a mumbling, senile nuisance.

Plays about families, perhaps more than others, reflect changes in social attitudes to family groups. Plays, and other literature might even affect these attitudes. If today, for instance, there are more relationships like Geoffrey's and Billy's in *Billy Liar* than the relationship of Rafe and his family, have the changes been necessarily for the better?

9

Hobson's Choice

Harold Brighouse

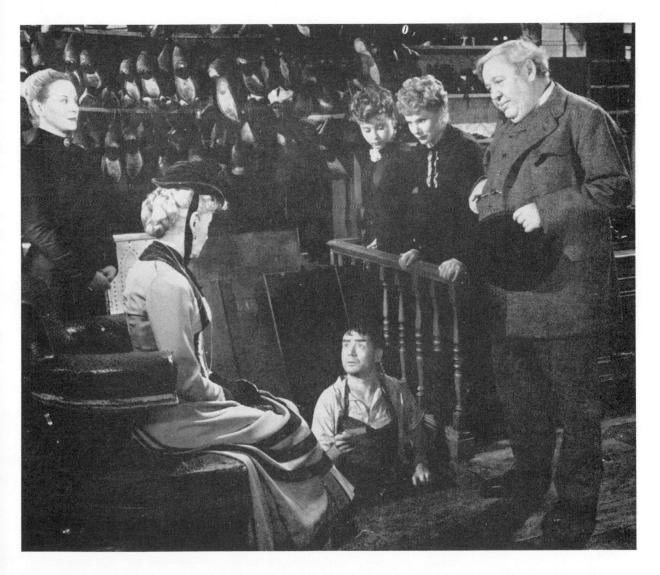

Hobson's World

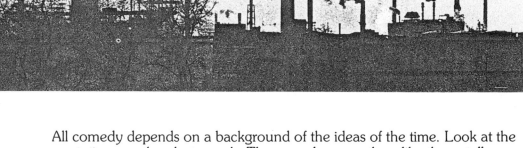

'I'm British middle class and proud of it. I stand for common sense.'

'You forget the majesty of trade and the unparalleled virtues of the British Constitution which are all based on the sanity of the middle classes.'

'You can't marry Willie Mossop. Why, lass, his father was a workhouse brat.'

'And when me and Willie are richer than the lot of you put together, it'll be a grand satisfaction to look back and think about how we were when we began.'

'I'll choose a pair of husbands for my girls.'

'Mostly my daughters do as I bid them, and the missus does the leathering, if they don't.'

'What's she want to praise a workman to his face for? Making them uppish.'

All comedy depends on a background of the ideas of the time. Look at the quotations on the photograph. These, and many others like them, tell us:

1 That daughters were expected to obey their fathers completely.
2 That workmen were expected to know their place.
3 That there was a strong class structure.

So if the daughter of a proud middle-class tradesman forced one of her father's workmen to marry her and set up a rival business that destroyed his, she would be breaking all the 'rules'. The result would be conflict – a humorous conflict.

This is the basis of Hobson's Choice.

Willie Mossop

Find quotations to show how Willie is looked down on as Hobson's serving man. Find what the other characters, particularly Hobson, say about him. Why might he first appear from a cellar below stage?

Read this piece from a review of a performance of the play:

> The . . . hit of the show, however, is Andrew Robertson's Mossop. He does have a lot in his favour, to be sure, but this is a performance that never wallows in the advantages. Emerging like some timid animal from the Hobson workroom, his demeanour is that of a seriously deprived individual whose hands might nevertheless have in them the distinctive skill of a master craftsman. To convey this from the eyes, and from the slightly cringing posture, while dealing with the obvious looks of the male who is softest putty in a woman's palm, is acting on a subtle scale . . .
>
> *London Theatre Record*

Directing the actor

Imagine that you are the director. How would you advise Willie to act? Write it down act by act, telling the actor the changes you want him to make as he goes through the play.

Imagine what it was like

Workmen were probably treated even worse in the country than in the town. Read this account by a gardener in a stately home:

I went to Lordship's when I was fourteen and stayed for fourteen years. There were seven gardeners and goodness knows how many servants in the house. It was a frightening experience for a boy. Lord and Ladyship were very, very, very Victorian and very domineering. It was 'Swing your arms' every time they saw us. Ladyship would appear suddenly from nowhere when one of us boys were walking to fetch something. 'Swing your arms!' she would shout. We wore green baize aprons and collars and ties no matter how hot it was, and whatever we had to do had to be done on the dot. Nobody was allowed to smoke. A gardener was immediately sacked, if he was caught smoking, no matter how long he had worked there.

We must never be seen from the house; it was forbidden. And if people were sitting on the terrace or on the lawn, and you had a great barrow-load of weeds, you might have to push it as much as a mile to keep out of view . . . you felt like somebody with a disease . . .

from *Akenfield* by Ronald Blythe

Imagine you are the boy gardener and you see a performance of *Hobson's Choice*. Describe your joy in diary form, or as you talk to someone, as you see Willie triumph over his master. Imagine it was your first visit to a theatre. Look at the pictures on pages 134 and 139 to 140 to help you with the atmosphere.

Discussion

These two photographs from a production show the rise of Willie and the fall of Hobson. Decide the precise points in the play each represents.

Discuss what the faces and posture of each of the three characters in both scenes show in their feelings at the precise moments.

Writing

Write what you think each character should be feeling at that stage and say how well you think each is expressing that feeling by facial expression and posture.

Maggie

Read this piece by Jane. Discuss it and then write the advice you would give
to the actress taking the part, if you were the director:

The Role of Maggie in Hobson's Choice

I should think Maggie is a difficult part to play for an actress, she would have to get it out just right.

You start off by not liking her very much when she does not let her sister see Albert. We are also told by her father that she is an old maid so she must not look too young. I also think she should not be pretty. Vicky is the pretty one so Maggie must look a bit plain. Perhaps glasses would help, if they had glasses in those days.

She must be strong in character as when she proposes to Willie. I suppose you would call her a feminist in the way she stands up to her father and organises her own life.

The difficult bits are the scenes with Willie. She has to bully him and make him a man who can stand up for himself, yet we have got to like her. The scene where she takes him off by the ear would have to be got just right. It would be no good making her sexy in this scene.

I think that in the beginning we have got to see her as a cold, scheming character, but as the play goes on she gets warmer as it were and we like her more. She would have to speak with a Lancashire accent, a posh voice would be no good. Yet she would have to speak without so much dialect as Willie.

How well has Jane understood the role of Maggie? What other things would
you add? Are there any parts that are wrong or where she has not expressed
herself clearly?

A critic's view of Maggie

This is what one critic said about a performance of Maggie. An actress called Penelope Keith took the part.

> Tidying up inconvenient people as she bustles around the stage . . .
>
> Penelope Keith – huge, ramrod-spined, selflessly dowdy and charmless – is rather wonderful as the practical-minded spinster who unearths her cobbler husband quite literally below stairs and drags him off to the wedding bed by the ear.
>
> All that she lacks is the vulnerability of a woman who realises that, if ever she is to get a husband, she must snatch at him – and to hell with dignity.
>
> Miss Keith, looking severe and practical, allows her chin to sink deeper and deeper into her chest as she prepares to pulverize her male victims . . .
>
> *London Theatre Record*

Is this the way you thought Maggie should be played? Discuss your views in class.

Hobson

Hobson is the pompous character brought down that audiences love to see in plays and films.

What I don't like about Hobson

Use quotations to show how the author makes him unlikeable in Act One. Show, too, how he ill-treats his daughters. Why, at the end of the play in Act Four, might you feel a bit sorry for him? Again you are the director. What advice would you give to the actor on how to play the last act?

Conflict in plays

In a play, whether serious or comic, you need to have conflict between the characters, otherwise there is no play. If Maggie had not faced up to Hobson but had just agreed with him you would have nothing to interest you.

Write the arguments

1 What are the arguments between:
   Maggie and Hobson,
   Hobson and Alice and Vicky,
   Maggie and Albert,
   Maggie and Ada,
   Hobson and Dr MacFarlane,
   Hobson and Willie,
   Alice and Vicky?
   Do not use quotes but write down in your own words what they argue about.

2 Write these imaginary conflict scenes in play form:
   a) Willie being told off by a schoolmaster for being dull when he was younger. Willie tries to defend himself.
   b) Maggie being offered poor goods (say vegetables) in a shop.
   c) Hobson being teased by Jim Heeler in the Moonraker's about Maggie's marriage.

Two themes explored

Drink

At the time the play was written there were several movements like The Band of Hope who campaigned against the evils of strong drink.

Discussion

Is the play partly an attempt to preach against the evils of drink? Do you find drunks funny on the stage or on TV? How drunk or hung over should Hobson be in Act Three? What do you think of Hobson's speech in Act Four beginning: 'Much use forbidding is. I've had my liquor for as long as I can remember . . .'?

Feminism

Many playwrights at the turn of the century were interested in the role of women in society. Bernard Shaw wrote *Major Barbara* and *Man and Superman*. Ibsen wrote *A Doll's House*.

Discussion

How does the play support a woman's right to determine her own future? How would you criticize Hobson for his attitude to women? Is Willie a fitting husband for Maggie? What advances for women have been made since the play was written? For instance, despite Maggie's character, is she developing Willie to be master of the house and of her? Look for evidence of this.

Further study activities

Looking at dramatic moments

The photographs below and on page 140 each represent a dramatic moment in the play. Choose one (and possibly photostat it for your folder) and give it a suitable caption. Say precisely what is happening at that moment, identifying both the characters and the situation. Say how effectively you think the scene emphasises the drama of the moment and how well you think the actors and actresses are showing their feelings by facial expression and posture.

Writing

1 Write the letter Maggie wrote to Mrs Hepworth asking for help, *or* write, as a play, about when she visited her and asked for money. (Willie could go as well.)

2 Write the advertising letter Maggie sends out to advertise Mossop and Hobson, the new boot shop, including a recommendation from Mrs Hepworth.

3 Say why *Hobson's Choice* is an anti-drink play and then write a short anti-drink play of your own about a teenager who drinks.

Organising the production

1 You are the make-up artist for a young cast for the play (say a school production). How would you make up: Hobson, Maggie, and Willie? You can use false hair, padding, nose putty, face lines, etc. Use both drawings and descriptions.

2 You have to direct this play at your school. Write, as for the programme, the problems you had in staging the play. Think about casting, scenery and its changes, lighting, costumes, the accents needed by the actors and properties.

3 Design a programme and write an advertisement for your school production. What parts would you emphasise to attract customers?

10

An Inspector Calls

J. B. Priestley

The author's beliefs and aims

J. B. Priestley journeyed about England a great deal. He put down his thoughts about his travels in a book called *English Journey*. From train windows he had seen the mess industry and its slag tips had made of Britain. He wrote:

As I thought of some of the places I had seen, Wolverhampton and St Helen's and Bolton and Gateshead and Jarrow and Shotton, I remembered a book I had just read, in which we are told to return as soon as possible to sturdy Victorian individualism. But for my part I felt like calling back a few of those sturdy individualists simply to rub their noses in the nasty mess they had made. Who gave them leave to turn this island into an ashpit? . . . Damn you, I'm all right: you can see as much written in black letters across half England . . .

By 'sturdy Victorian individualism' Priesley is referring to Victorian capitalism when a man could build a factory or dig a mine anywhere in order to make money. Much of Britain is scarred by this legacy of uncontrolled building and development. There were also no anti-pollution regulations in those days. Arthur Birling is a capitalist and an industrialist in the Victorian mould. Priestley believes he has also risen to success by exploiting his workers, paying them a poor wage. His attitude is summed up early in the play:

'. . . may we look forward to the time when Crofts and Birlings are no longer competing but working together – for lower costs and higher prices . . .'

'. . . and I've learned in the good hard school of experience – that man has to mind his own business and look after himself and his own . . . .'

The Birling household

As the curtain rises on the play about the Birlings we see a comfortable, well-furnished dining room. We can tell by the drinks and cigars and the dress of the actors that these are well-off people. A servant also appears and we learn that they have a cook to stress their wealth.

Writing

Read pages 1–10 (Longman edition). Write paragraphs of 5 to 6 lines in answer to these questions:

1　Are the family happy?

2　Are there any signs of rifts or potential disagreements?

3　What is the relationship between Birling and his wife?

4　What is the relationship between Birling and his children?

5　Are the family prosperous from what they say as well as from what we see?

6　If Birling is wrong about matters of fact, he is perhaps wrong about matters of opinion. How does the author make it clear that Birling is wrong about matters of fact?

7　How does Birling show 'the sturdy individualism' that Priestley despises? How is this individualism shown to be smug and selfish?

8　What is the class difference between the Birlings and Gerald? How does Birling show his awareness of this?

Direct the actors

Imagine you are to direct *An Inspector Calls* for a school play. Write the speech you would make to the actors and actresses about the way they should act their parts in pages 1–10. Pick out particular lines you would like them to stress to show their characters.

Before you begin discuss in pairs these comments by a director of the play: 'Obviously I must achieve in the first moments of the play a feeling of normality. An average family and quite a nice one . . . The play should be cast sympathetically so that the audience is on the side of the people.'
Why is this director anxious to play down the nastier side of the Birlings before the Inspector arrives?
Is it better that the audience is quite shocked to find that people who seemed quite normal and nice have done nasty things in their lives, or should the play show the Birlings for what they are from the very start? (There are enough clues.) Make it clear in your speech to your actors which approach you favour.

Act it out

In groups of five, with one person acting as the
director, present this piece of the play (page 3,
Longman edition):

Sheila	(*half serious, half playful*) Yes – except for all last summer, when you never came near me, and I wondered what had happened to you.
Gerald	And I've told you – I was awfully busy at the works all that time.
Sheila	(*same tone as before*) Yes, that's what *you* say.
Mrs Birling	Now, Sheila, don't tease him. When you're married you'll realize that men with important work to do sometimes have to spend nearly all their time and energy on their business. You'll have to get used to that, just as I had.
Sheila	I don't believe I will. (*Half playful, half serious, to Gerald.*) So you be careful.
Gerald	Oh – I will, I will.
	Eric suddenly guffaws. His parents look at him.
Sheila	(*severely*) Now – what's the joke?
Eric	I don't know – really. Suddenly I felt I just had to laugh.
Sheila	You're squiffy.
Eric	I'm not.
Mrs Birling	What an expression, Sheila! Really, the things you girls pick up these days!
Eric	If you think that's the best she can do –
Sheila	Don't be an ass, Eric.
Mrs Birling	Now stop it, you two. Arthur, what about this famous toast of yours?

Present it in two different ways:

1 Making the piece seem like normal friendly banter of a happy family.

2 Making the piece show that there are rifts and antagonisms below the seemingly happy surface of the Birling household before the Inspector arrives.

NB: The author's stage direction (*half serious, half playful*) for Sheila's first line shows he wants a balance between the two moods, but you should try the difference that tipping the balance first to one side and then the other makes.

Before you begin your rehearsals consider:

1 What gestures can be made to show the difference between anger and playfulness?

2 How do you interpret: 'Eric suddenly guffaws'. Is he really drunk, loud and sneering?

3 The way these lines are said is particularly important:
   'And I've told you'
   'So you be careful'
   'Oh – I will, I will'
   'You're squiffy'
   'What an expression'
   'Don't be an ass, Eric'
   'Now stop it, you two'

Learn your lines before you start – the maximum is eight, for Mrs Birling.

Draw the set

Draw or paint the set using the picture on page 141 to get the feel of the period. The room should be as big as possible for a stage, with a high ceiling and possibly a chandelier. The furniture should be of the period, for example red-plush seats. The fireplace could have red or green tiles and would be big. The window curtains would hang to the floor. Lighting would probably be by gas. The wallpaper could be heavily patterned.

The Inspector's visit

'The play begins with all the main protagonists together (all the main parts), and then separates them out for individual attention of the Inspector.' This suits Priestley's dramatic purpose which he says is: 'to have a continuous and varied series of little scenes within your big drama'.

Discuss in groups

Why does the Inspector interrogate each of the family separately? Why does he not show the photograph to them all at the same time? Could there be more than one girl who has died?

Spotlight on Birling

1 What is found out?

2 How does he react?

3 What are the reactions of the other characters to the revelations? (Are they supportive, shocked or critical?)

Spotlight on Sheila

1 What tale does Sheila tell?

2 How does she react to her own revelations?

3 How do you feel about her behaviour to Eva Smith?

Spotlight on Gerald

1 What does Gerald reveal?

2 How does Sheila react?

3 How do Mr and Mrs Birling react?

4 What are our feelings towards Gerald on his engagement night?

Spotlight on Mrs Birling

1 What is found out?

2 Why did Mrs Birling refuse Eva help?

3 Why does she not accept the blame?

4 Why is Eric's entrance dramatic?

Spotlight on Eric

1 What does Eric reveal?

2 What does he accuse his mother of?

3 Why is this a very dramatic scene?

4 How does Mrs Birling react to the revelations?

A diagram of the characters

Write in the boxes how each of the characters
is connected to Eva Smith.

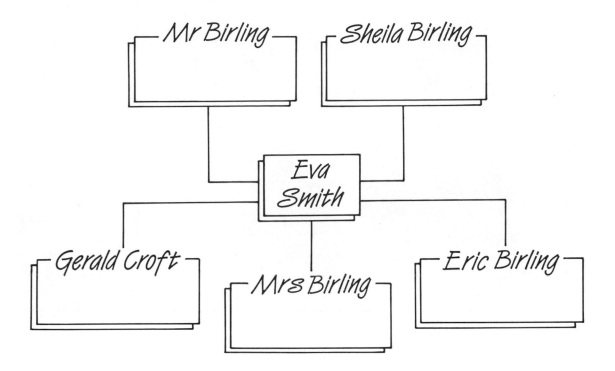

The aftermath

Read the Inspector's speech (page 54, Longman edition):

Inspector   But just remember this. One Eva Smith has gone – but there are
millions and millions and millions of Eva Smiths and John Smiths
still left with us, with their lives, their hopes and fears, their
suffering and chance of happiness, all intertwined with our lives,
with what we think and say and do. We don't live alone. We are
members of one body. We are responsible for each other. And I
tell you that the time will soon come when, if men will not learn
that lesson, then they will be taught it in fire and blood and
anguish. Good night.

What does the Inspector want the family to learn from his visit? What was the
purpose of his visit? Is there any hope that it has had the desired effect?

Are the characters changed?

To what extent are the characters changed by the Inspector's visit? Use quotations. Here are some to help you:

Birling   I was almost certain for a knighthood in the next Honour's List. There's every excuse for what both your mother and I did.

Mrs Birling   He certainly didn't make me confess – as you call it. I told him quite plainly that I thought I had done my duty.
The rude way he spoke to Mr Birling and me – it was quite extraordinary.

Gerald   Well, you were right. There wasn't any such Inspector. We've been had.
What do you make of this business now? Was it a hoax?

Eric   Well, I don't blame you. But don't forget I'm ashamed of you as well – yes, both of you.
He was our police inspector all right.

Sheila   You're pretending everything's just as it was before.
I tell you – whoever that Inspector was, it was anything but a joke. You knew that then. You began to learn something. And now you've stopped. You're ready to go on in the same way.

Further study activities

Discussion

1 Who is Inspector Goole? Is there any clue in his name?

> Birling That man definitely wasn't a police inspector at all.
>
> Eric He was our police inspector all right.

Who might the second inspector be? (Priestley, writing about students of his works said: 'Oddly enough they never asked about the second Inspector who was on his way, though this simply is not a dramatic twist but really the key to the play'.)

2 Using quotations from his speeches show what kind of a world the Inspector believes in. How far do the Birlings fall short of this world?

3 Would you blame one character more than another for Eva's death?

Writing

1 Write the diary of Eva Smith including all the events in the play. Ask your teacher for help if you are having trouble with the sequence of events.

2 Write, as a play, the scene with Sheila in the dress shop. (Imagine the dress was one of those on page 148.)

Design a programme

Look at the programme cover on this page. How successful is it in suggesting what the play is about? Design one of your own that gives the message of the play. Write down why you have designed it the way you have.

What do you think?

Write about your own reactions to the play as you read through it, listened to it, or watched it performed. What surprised you about it? What twists and turns did you not expect? What did you think of the ending?

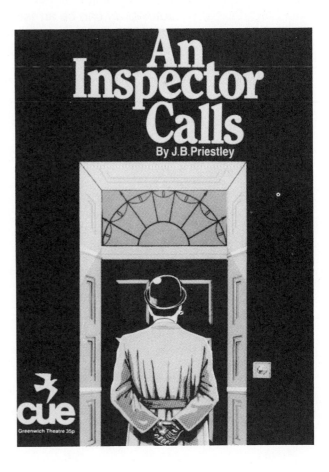

149

Look at the criticism

Read this criticism written by a student:

Nothing happens during the play. We find out a lot of things that have happened, all the characters' involvements with Eva Smith, but we don't see them happening. The play would have been more dramatic if it had shown some of these scenes. If we had seen Birling sacking Eva, or the scene in the dress shop, for instance, we would have disliked the characters even more.

But the play is set in the Birling's house, there is no variety in the setting and not much in the characters. One after another is shown to have treated Eva Smith badly, so that there is a sameness about them that eventually becomes boring.

The main weakness in the play, however, is the character of the Inspector. He acts like an Inspector, but you are never convinced he really is one, and nobody is surprised when it is discovered that he is a fake. Nothing happens as a result of his visit, because nothing can happen. The Birlings haven't done anything criminal. They have been thoughtless, selfish and even cruel, but nobody can be arrested for that.

If you have a play that seems like an investigation of a crime, you should have a crime, an arrest and punishment. Otherwise the audience feels cheated.

Write a response to the criticisms in this piece. Discuss and make notes on these questions before you begin:

1 Would it have helped if some of the scenes in which Eva Smith was ill-treated had been included? Which ones would be possible? What problems would their inclusion bring?

2 The first paragraph implies that the play isn't dramatic enough because these scenes have been left out. What are the dramatic parts of the play? Why is it untrue to say that nothing happens in the play?

3 Consider the advantages Priestley has gained by setting the play in one room. Are there any disadvantages?

4 The writer says that the characters aren't varied enough because they have all done the same things – treated Eva Smith cruelly. Why is it unfair to say they have no real variety?

5 Consider the last paragraph. The writer is suggesting that the audience, as well as the Birlings, have been deceived. What advantages does Priestley gain by using the format of a criminal investigation? How does this format show the author's own strong feelings about the Birlings and people like them?

Making a film

A film director might consider showing, in flashback, the scenes in which the Birlings ill-treated Eva Smith. (Why is it much easier in a film to do this?)

Choose two of the scenes not shown in the play and write the dialogue for them. Try to keep faith in Priestley's characters, their manner as well as the matter of their speeches. If you wish you may include directions for the camera, e.g. what shots to show in close-up and how the actors move.

Wider reading

An Inspector Calls gives you the opportunity to look at a particular type of crime novel known as 'The Whodunnit' so popular that it is almost written to a formula. In it the reader is invited to guess from clues 'who did the murder' with suspense being maintained until the last chapter. Read one of the novels by Agatha Christie or Dorothy L. Sayers. See how Priestley has used the formula in making each character a suspect in turn. His twist, however, in exposing hypocrisy, is that 'they all dunnit'.

11

Z for Zachariah

Robert O'Brien

Science–fantasy

Ann Burden's small valley is one of the last places on Earth where anyone can live. After the destruction brought by the hydrogen bomb in what must have been the last war for mankind it is a lonely place. Family, neighbours, the rule of law, all those things that made up civilisation have disappeared.

Nevertheless, Ann, just coming up to her sixteenth birthday, manages to survive. She is capable; she cares for the animals left on her parents' farm. She does not waste time being sorry for herself. She has some hope for the future and even still a belief in God.

Into her world, looking alien in his survival suit, comes John Loomis, a scientist. He has new ideas which might have made life easier for him and Ann. They might have drawn strength from each other's company but Loomis is self-obsessed and selfish. That brings disaster.

The book is fascinating in many ways, the most obvious of which is its element of science–fantasy. What would you do if you were one of the last survivors of a nuclear war? How could you live? *Z for Zachariah* gives an answer to questions like that. It also presents the old and intriguing theme of a person left alone in an unpeopled world. Ann's valley is a kind of desert island. Like Robinson Crusoe, it is only by her own efforts that she stays alive. Nor is there any help on its way for Ann. The human being who finds her comes as a threat.

Then, from that first moment of fear when Ann sees the smoke from the approaching traveller's distant fire, the story itself moves along compellingly in a series of gripping incidents. Yet another aspect of the book lies in the moral questions it seems to raise. Who is better equipped to survive in Ann Burden's world, the educated scientist, planning and scheming for self-survival or the ill-educated but kindhearted girl? Which of them deserves to survive?

Detailed study of the text

The text has been divided up into eight sections of about three chapters each. The chapter numbers are given with each section.

The coming of the stranger

(chapters 1 to 3)

Discussion

Is Ann Burden rather lucky? What problems would real survivors of a nuclear war have to cope with? Would they find food and water easily? Would a Geiger counter solve any of their problems?

Sketch maps

1 Using the information given in these chapters and your own imagination, draw a sketch map of the valley, labelling such places as the farm, the store, the cave and so on.

2 Using the information in the chapters and your imagination, draw a sketch map of the country round the valley, labelling things like Claypole Ridge, Ogdentown and the direction of Dean Town. Mark out the probable route Loomis took to Burden valley.

Illustrations

1 Draw (or describe in detail) what you think Loomis looked like when he was wearing his survival suit.

2 Choose a scene you think would make a good illustration to this chapter and draw or describe it in detail.

Diary

As if you were Loomis, write his day's entry for a diary for May 24th, the day he reached the valley. You can use the detail given in chapter 3.

Role play

Mr and Mrs Burden, Mr and Mrs Klein, the storekeepers, Ann's cousin David and her brother Joseph all went on a second trip to discover what had happened to other people. They were going to visit the Amish – a peace-loving and very religious farming community – and then intended to travel through Baylor to the large town of Dean Town. Discuss what they might have found and decide what happened to them. Was it an accident or an attack of radiation sickness? Then act out their conversation as they talk about what they have seen and as they realise they are not going to get back to the valley.

News report

'. . . there were only a few people left where he was and not much food.'

What was happening in the town where the radio announcer was? (You will find the paragraph about the last radio station in chapter 1.) Were people fighting each other for food? Were people dying of wounds or radiation sickness? Write, as if you were the announcer, a news report about the place and what was happening there.

Ann Burden

In her diary Ann Burden is speaking directly to the reader. What opinion do you have of her from the first chapters? If you met her for the first time like this would you like her or would you have some criticisms of her? Say what you think of her, giving some evidence from these chapters to justify your view of her.

Making contact with the stranger (chapters 4 and 5)

Film or video presentation

Ann tells us much of what she feels. How could you translate the diary into scenes and dialogue for a video or film? Would you have to cut things out and select? What incidents in these two chapters are needed to carry the story along? Discuss what makes a film interesting. Would, for instance, a long sequence of Loomis walking up the valley be suitable or not? After discussion, make up a storyboard, listing the scenes you have chosen to shoot and what happens in them.

Faro's tale

How had the dog survived? How did he feel when he saw human beings again? Write an account as if you were the dog, Faro.

Thinking like Loomis

As if you were Loomis, write out what his thoughts might have been as he explored the valley and got new clothes from the store.

Ann Burden

Ann, at this stage in the story, knows nothing about Loomis or what is going to happen. Is she sensible or cowardly to hide from the stranger? If you think she is sensible, give your reasons. If not, discuss what else she might have done.

Radiation sickness (chapters 6 to 10)

Script writing

A film or video would have to translate the diary form of the book into actual scenes with dialogue. Write in play form the scene where Loomis is told about the survival suit by Professor Kylmer (details in chapter 6) and then the scene where Loomis stops Edward leaving the shelter. There are some details about this at the end of chapter 7. You are only given Loomis's side of the argument but may be able from that to work out what Edward might have said.

Plans for progress

At this stage it seems that Loomis might be of help. List the ideas he has to improve conditions on the farm for their future.

Hallucinations

What was in Loomis's mind when, in his fever, he ran out of the house with the gun? Where did he think he was? Who was he firing at? Edward? Write, as if you were Loomis, the thoughts that might have been going through his head at the time.

Loomis

At this stage in the book, what is your impression of Loomis? Does he show any signs of his selfish nature? How helpful is he to Ann? Is he fair to her about her part in not warning him about the water he swam in? Give your opinion of him along with evidence about him that has led to that opinion.

Ann Burden

Loomis's illness makes life more difficult for Ann. In her place would you have done all that she did for Loomis? If so, list the things she did, saying why each was necessary and sensible. If not, point out the things you would not have done, saying why.

Recovery (chapters 11 to 13)

Discussion – trial by the survivors

You are a group of survivors who have learned how Loomis killed Edward. You could appoint someone to present the case against Loomis and a counsel for his defence. (Ann gives some points in his defence towards the end of chapter 12.) Say what you can for and against Loomis and decide what you think should happen to him.

Looking after the invalid

You are alone in a house with someone who, like Loomis, is unconscious, feverish and very ill. You can't get out for help and you have no telephone. You have no medical books but you do have a copy of *Z for Zachariah*. What do you do for the sick person, following Ann's example? Are there some things you wouldn't do? What might you have in the house to help that Ann doesn't have?

Getting to know Mr Loomis
(chapters 14 to 16)

Birthday

In Ann's position, what sort of birthday would
you have had? Can you cook? Bake bread? Or
would you have to rely on tins from the store?
Describe your birthday meal.

Books

If you were a survivor, like Ann or Loomis, but
could get into Ogdenstown, which ten books
would you bring back? Say briefly why.

Loomis

1 Loomis is irritated with Ann about her visit
to the church and when she mentions the
suit. He is secretive about trying to walk.
What might he be feeling and planning
during the fortnight? Write about it, in
either diary form or as if you were thinking
to yourself.

2 How did other people, his parents, his
cousin, the people he worked with in the
Navy and at Cornell University feel about
Loomis? Choose three or four of them.
Give each a name. Say whether they were
a relative, a friend, or a workmate of
Loomis and give their opinion of Loomis as
if you were the person.

Discussion – survival

You are survivors of a nuclear war but you
have enough preserved food, clothing and
shelter for the moment. You also have seeds.
How many of you would know what and when
to plant and what sort of crops you might grow
here in Britain to help your survival? Would
some of you be satisfied if you could do no
more than that? You can give what you think
might be your own personal responses to the
situation. Would some of you want to set up a
more technological situation? If so, how would
you go about it? What sort of technology
would you first try to set up?
You might discuss the individual choice of
books made under 'Books' above.

Flight to the cave
(chapters 17 to 19)

Master of the house

Loomis seems to see Ann as almost his property or even a kind of slave. List some of the things he says or does before the attack which suggest this.

Loomis

Read the end of chapter 19 again. Then, as if you were Loomis, write in diary form or as if you were thinking to yourself, his plans to recapture Ann.

Ann in danger (chapters 20 to 23)

Winners and losers

During the days from July 1st to August 4th, Ann feels she is in a game of 'move-counter-move, like a chess game'. Using what happens in the chapter, work out the winning and losing moves on each side.
Draw this in your book, adding squares as you need them:

Ann			
Loomis			

Decide which happenings are a win for Ann or Loomis and write 'Win' in the appropriate box with a number. Then write a numbered sentence below the boxes to describe what happened. You might begin like this:

	1	2	
Ann	Win	Win	
Loomis			

1 She has supplies in the cave.

2 She can build a fireplace for cooking.

3 She does the work on the farm. (Is this a win for Ann or one for Loomis?)

4 Loomis finds he can use the tractor. (Is this a win for Loomis or is it not important enough to mention?)

You might discuss your choice of wins and losses with a partner or work in a group on this.

Escape route

Use your map or draw another one and mark on it the route Ann took on the tenth day to deceive Loomis about the position of the cave. You will find the incident near the beginning of chapter 21. Put also on the map Ann's escape route and where she hid when Loomis came up to discover the cave.

Discussion

In Ann's position, would you have done exactly what she did? Or would you have tried to stop Loomis? How? With a gun? By locking the store before he did? Would there be peaceful ways of stopping him? If not, you might go on to discuss whether there are situations in which one nation simply has to go to war with another or whether people are sometimes justified in using violence against each other.

Defeat for Loomis (chapters 24 to 26)

Discussion

'I was convinced . . . that Mr Loomis was insane.'

Is this true? Are there reasons for thinking that he saw his behaviour as normal and sensible? Could he have his reasons for seeing Ann as just a silly, frightened, young girl? Does his work on the farm after Ann has been driven from her cave suggest insanity or a fairly ordinary – if selfish – state of mind? If he is mad, is this a complete excuse for what he has done?

Childhood

As Ann passes her house for the last time, she remembers happy evenings there with her family before the war. Describe what might have happened during one of these evenings. (Ann mentions some things towards the end of chapter 25.)

Loomis at work

In chapter 25 Ann sees Loomis cultivating the ground. What other sort of work might he have been doing in and around the house? She hears him hammering. What might he have been making? A prison for her? Write about some of the jobs you think Loomis might have been working on.

Loomis alone

What would Loomis think about after he saw Ann leave the valley? Would he regret what he had done? Would he be afraid? Would he make plans? As if you were Loomis write about his state of mind then.

Ann's story

Is the end of the diary the end of Ann? Or did she find the children she dreamed about? What was it like to travel through the 'deadness'? Continue the tale, either in diary form, writing as if you were Ann or as a story, choosing your own happy or unhappy ending.

The cover of the book

1 Draw or describe what picture you would put on the cover of this book.

2 Publishers usually write a short description of a book to go on or inside its cover. This tells a little of the story, or mentions an exciting incident. It is intended to make readers want to buy and read the book. Write your own short description of this book.

Discussion

1 Are you sorry for Ann Burden at the end of the book or are you pleased that, in a way, she has won? Say how you feel about her, describing those things about her character and behaviour that have made you feel that way.

2 Do you think Loomis might not have been so bad, if there had not been a nuclear war? Using some of the things he does and says to illustrate your answer, give your opinion of him.

3 Would life for a survivor of a nuclear war be easier or harder than the picture you get of it in this book? Give your views on this, mentioning things in the book as evidence for those views.

4 Pick a) the most exciting, b) the saddest, and c) the happiest moments in the book, and explain why you have picked those particular episodes.

Write a radio script

Choose an occasion in the book when Ann and Loomis are together. Write out what happens as a radio script. Make your script about two or three pages long. Write what is said by Ann and Loomis in the form of a play. You can use a narrator to explain what is happening when no one is talking and, as in a radio production, you will need to mention the sound effects to be used.

Wider reading

Two of the topics in *Z for Zachariah* are life after a major catastrophe and survival in a new and unknown world. Here are some other books in which those topics occur.

Living after a catastrophe:
When the Wind Blows – Raymond Briggs;
On the Beach – Nevil Shute;
Empty World – John Christopher;
Threads – Barry Hines;
Ridley Walker – Russell Hoban.

This last one is difficult to read since it is written in the kind of language Russell Hoban imagines people might speak 'after The Bomb'. It is a weird, gripping story, though, and worth struggling with.

Survival:
Walkabout – James Vance Marshall;
The short story 'A Man Called Horse' in the book *Indian Country* by Dorothy M Johnson;
Poems: 'Your Attention Please' – Peter Porter;
       'The Unexploded Bomb' – C Day Lewis.

12

The Stories of
Roald Dahl

The short story

A novel can tell us about the lives of many characters and the many things that happen to them over the years. There is more than one kind of short story but in most, as the short story does not have the space of a novel, we meet only a few characters and learn about possibly one event, one change in their lives. A short story writer must compress, concentrate, pick out only those details that carry the story along.

In each of these Roald Dahl stories there are few people; two in 'The Hitchhiker' and 'The Landlady', three in 'Mrs Bixby and the Colonel's Coat'. There are more in 'Skin' and 'The Champion of the World' but, even in these tales, there are no more than three or four main characters.

The basic idea around which the main happening in the story revolves is not complicated. One story answers the question: 'What was the murder weapon and where is it hidden?' Another asks: 'How does the hitchhiker show his gratitude?', and yet another, 'How did Perkins revenge himself on a bully?'

Details are carefully selected. The narrator in 'Galloping Foxley' tells us not his life story but only that part of it which concerns Foxley. That is really all that is essential to lead us to the mistake that is made at the end of the story. We know nothing much about Billy in 'The Landlady' except that he is seventeen and fairly innocent – which makes him an ideal victim for the sinister landlady. In 'Mrs Bixby and the Colonel's Coat' where Dahl seems to be putting off the start of his story by writing a little four-paragraph essay about American women and their husbands, we find that little essay is necessary since it prepares us to sympathise with Mr Bixby rather than his wife even though he has deceived her.

It all sounds simple but there is a craftiness or craft about it. The effect of the story comes from the way that it is told and the writer's gift for words. Dahl intrigues us by starting 'Galloping Foxley' years after the event and brings the story closer to us by letting the man to whom it happened tell it. 'The Champion of the World' is also more striking and immediate by being told by one of the characters in the story. 'Skin' and 'The Landlady' are more gripping because their god-like narrator knows more about what is happening in the tale than any of the characters can guess.

Not all short story writers write short stories like Roald Dahl's. Those of D. H. Lawrence or Chekhov are more about emotions than events. Rudyard Kipling's stories sometimes cover more ground, dealing with longer time spans and more characters. Many writers, however, such as 'Saki' (H. H. Munro), O. Henry, Guy de Maupassant or Somerset Maugham were adept at this form, this kind of short story in which carefully selected detail and skilfully crafted telling move the tale along like a lighted fuse to its – generally unexpected – conclusion.

Peculiar happenings and strange characters

In Roald Dahl's stories we come across some very peculiar happenings and some strange characters. All the stories are odd but some are odder than others. There are those that happen outside the world we know. A murderous landlady skilled in taxidermy is not part of everybody's experience.

Another group is closer to reality because the stories hinge on weird but credible characters. We may never have met a gambler with a chopping knife, an enormously skilful pickpocket or a man who will do anything to gain a valuable picture but when Roald Dahl describes them we don't doubt that they could exist.

Then there are stories of rats, of school and of murder which do appear to be part of reality in a way that an unusual or surprising news story can be.

So we don't question the reality of the stories while we are reading them. The matter-of-fact tone of voice in which they are told, the common place details carry us along. We are fascinated; we believe in this fantastic, blackly-humorous world of Roald Dahl.

Even when we have finished reading, we don't so much question the reality of that world as wonder about it. Roald Dahl might, just possibly, be giving us a picture of things as they are. There could be people like this about, cruel, greedy people who will stop at nothing to gain their ends. We have probably just been lucky. We have not met so many of them. As we wonder, the stories leave us with a disturbing thought. Will we go on being lucky? Or are some of Roald Dahl's sinister characters, as it were, lurking round the next corner, just waiting for us to come along?

Detailed study of the stories

The stories dealt with here are from the book *A Roald Dahl Selection* published by Longman. They are dealt with in the order in which they occur.

Man from the South

Film or video

Many of these stories appeared on television as *Tales of the Unexpected*. For this, the designer might have to plan two sets.

Draw, or sketch and label or describe what the swimming pool scene might look like and then do the same for the hotel room. The story itself gives you some details to work with so it will help if you look at it again. It will also help if you decide where the hotel is. Is it somewhere like Florida or the Bahamas?

The hand on the table

A high point of tension could be a camera shot of the young man's hand tied to the table. Using the story and your own imagination, sketch out how this hand was tied down.

Illustrations

Draw or describe in detail two moments in the story which you think would make good illustrations.

Spin-off stories

1 It seems that the narrator is a man. Is he young or old? Is he there on holiday or on business? What sort of work does he do? What does he look like? Why doesn't he try harder to stop the bet? Describe the sort of person you think he is.

2 As if you were the English girl, describe your thoughts as first the bet is made by the swimming pool and then your reactions in the hotel room.

3 How did the Man from the South start? Was he using a lighter himself one day and did that give him an idea? Or did someone have the same bet with him to start him off? Write a short account of how the idea of the bet began.

4 How did the Man meet his wife? Was he already married to her when he got the idea for the strange bet? Or did he meet her by betting with her? Write an account of their first meeting.

The scene in the surgery

After she lost each finger, the wife would have to go for treatment to a doctor or a hospital. Would she tell the doctor about the bet or would she lie about how she kept losing fingers for fear of the police being called in? What sort of questions might the doctor ask? Write in play form the conversation the two people might have.

Lamb to the Slaughter

News item

Write a short account of the death of Maloney as it might appear in a newspaper. Make up your own headline.

Play scenes

1 What did Maloney tell his wife? That he was leaving her? Did he mention another woman? Did Mary Maloney say anything at all? Write the scene.

2 Maloney was in love with another woman. She insisted that he should leave his wife. Maloney needed to be convinced. Write the scene between Maloney and this other woman.

3 Write the scene between the detective and Sam, the shopkeeper, where Sam is questioned about Mary Maloney's visit to the shop.

4 Are the police completely taken in by Mary Maloney's account of what happened or do they start to be suspicious of her? If so, does she confess or not? Write the scene where Mary Maloney is questioned for a second time.

Ground plan

The police would make a sketch or photograph of the room with a chalk line to show where the body was lying. Draw this ground plan.

The Landlady

A phone call

When Billy Weaver doesn't turn up at the office, the Branch Manager rings his home. Write in play form the kind of conversation that might go on with Billy's mother. Would she be worried enough to ring the police? If so, write her conversation with the police.

News item

Write the news story covering the disappearance of the other two young men, Mulholland and Temple. Give your story a headline.

Looking into the future

The landlady opened the door immediately and had a bed ready. Did she know Billy was coming? Did she use cards or a crystal ball to see into the future? Did she have some strange power to draw Billy to her house? Write about her and what was happening in the house before Billy rang the bell.

Film or video

If you were picking an actress to play the landlady for a film or a video, what sort of person would you look for? Describe the person, mentioning her height, her age, the sort of clothing she would have to wear and so on. You will find some details in the story. Describe, too, the sort of voice she would have and the way she would speak.

Clues

There are some hints from when Billy goes into the house that something strange is going to happen. List the moments in the story that could have given a warning to Billy.

Afterwards

1 Has someone seen Billy going into the house? Do the police come and interview the landlady? Do they search the house and find the preserved bodies of the three young men? Does the landlady convince them that Billy has left and that she has nothing to do with his disappearance? Write about what happens in the form of a play.

2 Does Billy's disappearance remain a complete mystery? Does another young man turn up at the house? Write the story up to his arrival.

The bodies

We know that the preserved bodies of the two other young men are on the third floor together. Are they in bed in their pyjamas? Or are they clothed and standing or sitting? Where does the landlady put Billy when she has finished preserving him? Describe how you think the bodies are posed.

The Champion of the World

Cast list

List the names of all the characters in the story, describing in a few words what each of them looks like and adding a comment about each person's personality.

Court case

Mr Hazel might bring a court case against Claud and Gordon for poaching. Using the 'Cast lists' as a basis for discussion, work out who might appear in this case as witnesses and what each might say. Would, for instance, Bessie Morgan not tell the truth to save her reputation and that of her husband, the vicar? How far would Charlie Kinch, the taxi-driver, go to save Claud and Gordon? What sort of tale might Claud and Gordon make up to defend themselves? You will need magistrates and two lawyers for the court case, one for the prosecution and one for the defence. Then act out the case as it might happen in court.

A play scene

Decide whether the vicar does or does not know about the help his wife gives Claud in hiding stolen pheasants. Then write the short play scene where she has to confess that her connection with the poachers has been discovered and that there will probably be a scandal affecting him.

Publicity material

You have made a film or video of this story. Now you have to produce some publicity material. You will need to pick one or two interesting moments from the story to show as illustrations. Draw or describe these. You will also need to write a very short description of the story to make people want to see the film or video. Write this, too.

Afterwards

At the end of the story, Gordon, the story-teller, has decided to get well out of the way. Does he go off alone or with Claud? Is he angry with Claud for getting him into possible trouble? Do they argue? Do they bump into Mr Hazel or the police? If so, what do they say when they are questioned about the pheasants? Continue the story, telling it as if you were Gordon.

Galloping Foxley

Mr Perkins

Do the people who travel with William Perkins, the story-teller, find him unfriendly? Do the people who work for him find him fussy? Write an opinion of him as if you were one of them.

Mr Fortesque

Do the story-teller and Mr Fortesque, the man who he thought was Foxley, get to like each other or not? In play-form, continue their conversation after the end of the story. Does the story-teller explain about Foxley? Is Mr Fortesque sympathetic?

Mr Foxley

Did Foxley go on terrorising and bullying people when he left school or did he get what he deserved? Write a short account of what happened to him.

Pain

Write a poem about the most painful event in the story.

Film or television

If you were turning this story into a film or video, how many scenes would you use? List and number short details of each one. (For instance, would number one be 'Railway Station'?)

Group discussion

Do the punishments that society hands out to criminals fit the crimes? Should some be changed? Should some be less severe? Should some be harsher?

Illustration

Describe or draw what you think would be the best illustration to this story.

Mrs Bixby and the Colonel's Coat

Cyril

Mrs Bixby thinks Cyril is 'small and neat and bony' and that he wears 'silly suits' and is unattractive to women. Write, as if you were Cyril, Cyril's secret opinion of Mrs Bixby.

Casting

As if you were making a film or video, describe or draw what these characters should look like: the Colonel, Miss Pulteney, Cyril, the pawnbroker. Describe, too, how they should act. Are they proud or shy, or quiet or loud-voiced? Read the story again to get the details about them to start you off.

Scenes for a script

1 Has Cyril been having a love affair with Miss Pulteney? What is her first name? Does Cyril tell her he has bought the six thousand dollar coat specially for her? Write in play form the scene where he gives her the fur coat. Try to bring out her amazement and delight.

2 How amazed is Cyril when he goes to the pawnbroker to find what the ticket has brought him? Does he try to hide his amazement, in case the pawnbroker doubts whether he is the real owner? Write the scene between Cyril and the pawnbroker.

Agony aunt

If Mrs Bixby tells Cyril that the mink coat is really hers, she will have to tell him about the Colonel and Cyril might then throw her out of the house. Mrs Bixby does not seem either to have money of her own or to be able to earn any. If she does not claim the coat, Miss Pulteney will keep it. Write a letter, as if you were Mrs Bixby, to an advice column in a paper or magazine, explaining things and asking what you should do.
You can also write a reply from the 'agony aunt' who runs the column, giving Mrs Bixby some advice.

The Colonel

Did the Colonel get bored with Mrs Bixby or did he find a new lady friend? Write, as if you were the Colonel and as if you were talking to a friend, your reasons for finishing with Mrs Bixby.

Group discussion

Did Mrs Bixby get just what she deserved? Or is Cyril deceitful so that he deserves an unfaithful wife? Is the Colonel rather heartless? Who is the most sympathetic character in the story? Who is the least sympathetic? Is Miss Pulteney really in love with Cyril or is she attracted by his money?

Skin

News item

Write the news item about the sale of the newly-discovered Soutine painting in Buenos Aires. Did people know that it was painted on human skin and will you mention this? Give your item a headline.

Josie

1 Write, as if you were Josie, your opinion of Soutine.

2 How was Josie killed during the war?

The picture

Invent a title for the picture on Drioli's back.

Chaim Soutine

Though the story is from Dahl's imagination, it seems that Soutine was a real person. Find out what you can about him.

Drioli and the stranger

Either write a paragraph or two explaining what happened to Drioli and saying who the stranger was, *or* continue the story up to the sale of the picture describing where the stranger took Drioli and what happened after that.

Drioli's day

Where was Drioli living? How did he get money? By begging? Describe how Drioli spent the day before he saw the picture in the gallery window.

Film or video

List the scenes, giving a brief description of each, that you would use if you were turning this story into a film or video.

The Ratcatcher

The ratcatcher's home

Draw or describe what you think the place where the ratcatcher lived would look like.

An animal man

The walk, the appearance, the way he talks all describe the ratcatcher in such a way as to make us think of a rat. Write about another person, describing him or her in a way that makes us think of a certain animal. It could be a pleasant or unpleasant one.

An illustration

Draw or describe what you think would be a striking illustration to this story.

The poison

Give your own explanation why none of the rats ate any of the ratcatcher's poisoned oats.

Play scene

In play form write the conversation the ratcatcher would have with Lady Leonora Benson when he went to the Manor to deal with her rats.

TV Times

Write a short account of the television play that might be made from the story, to advertise it in a TV magazine. Make your account as interesting as possible but do not give away the end of the story.

The Hitchhiker

The rich man

The story-teller is a writer. Is he Roald Dahl or someone else? Write a brief account of his life, saying how he started writing and what his big successes in books, film and television have been. If you think he is Roald Dahl and you know other Dahl books you might use actual details from Dahl's life.

Learning a trade

How do you learn to be a pickpocket? Does someone have to teach you or do you teach yourself? Do you need a friend to practise on? Write about your early days of learning pickpocketing as if you were the pickpocket in the story. Remember the man is rather proud of his cleverness and skill.

A poster

Design a poster for Derby Day or some other meeting which will draw big crowds, to warn people of the danger of pickpockets.

Play scene

Choose one of these characters: a) the policeman's sergeant who will be annoyed when the policeman reports that he has lost his notebook with the details of the speeding motorist, or b) the policeman's wife or friend who will listen sympathetically to the policeman's story.
Then write out in play form the conversation they have about the motorist and his hitchhiker and what happened afterwards.

The hitchhiker

Write your own story about a motorist who picks up a strange hitchhiker late at night.

Wider reading

Other writers have written short stories which, like Roald Dahl's, are about odd or bizarre happenings. Read some of these and they might lead you into reading different kinds of fantastic tales or into different kinds of short stories altogether. Here are the titles of some bizarre short stories together with the titles of the books in which they appear.

'The Truth About Pyecraft' in *Selected Short Stories* by H. G. Wells;
'Talking to the Pigman' in *Nuncle* by John Wain;
'Sredni Vashtar' in *Short Stories* by Saki;
'The Shout' in *The Shout and Other Stories* by Robert Graves;
'Mr Loveday's Little Outing' in *Work Suspended* by Evelyn Waugh;
'Rachel and the Angel' in *Rachel and the Angel and other stories* by Robert Westall.

For collections of fantastic stories, you can look in the anthologies: *The Magnet Book of Strange Tales* edited by Jane Russell, and the series of anthologies *Out of this World* which contain mainly science-fiction stories.
Here, too, is a list of the books where you will find more of Roald Dahl's stories:
Someone Like You
Kiss Kiss
Over to You
Switch Bitch
The Wonderful Story of Henry Sugar and six more

Living together – a sample theme

Many of the novels and plays in this book could be grouped together under the theme 'Living together' – the problems human beings have in living with each other on the planet:

Of Mice and Men
A Kestrel for a Knave
A Taste of Honey
Animal Farm
Spring and Port Wine
An Inspector Calls

Other books on this theme are:
Across the Barricades – Joan Lingard
Lord of the Flies – William Golding
To Kill a Mockingbird – Harper Lee

A poem will help you look at this theme from a different angle. Read this short poem by D. H. Lawrence:

People

I like people quite well
at a little distance.
I like to see them passing and passing
and going their own way,
especially if I can see their aloneness alive in them.
Yet I don't want them to come too near.
If they will only leave me alone
I can still have the illusion that there is room enough in the world.

The poem would provide you with a different angle on the theme of 'Living together'. Novels and plays tell a story. The story may be an illustration of a particular idea or theme, but it is always expressed in a series of events; there is always a plot of some kind and part of the interest is sustained by the reader or the audience waiting to know what happens next.

A poem is more often an expression of feeling, a record of a particular emotion that catches the reader's interest, not by 'What happens next?' but either by surprising him or her with the freshness of a new thought, or by clear expression of something the reader has thought of already, and perhaps not been able to put into words. Whether or not you share the poet's view that you only like people 'at a little distance' it sets you thinking about your own attitude to other people.

Any anthology of poetry will provide you with poems on the theme of 'Living together'. Find some for yourself either on this theme or as comparison pieces for the particular text you are studying.

Traditional titles for coursework

GCSE emphasises new approaches to literature, but does not intend the older ones to be discarded. Here are some questions that will enable you to respond to your texts in ways that demand detailed knowledge of the whole and are based on reference and quotation to support your views.

Of Mice and Men

1 'Of Mice and Men is a sad book, but one which re-inforces a belief in the goodness of people.' Do you agree?

2 'The weak, poor and unhappy always win Steinbeck's approval.' How far is this shown in Of Mice and Men?

3 'Of Mice and Men is about human nature, not about America at the time of the Depression.' Do you agree?

A Kestrel for a Knave

1 Show how Barry Hines uses description to give a vivid insight into what life was like in this Yorkshire town.

2 In what ways do you feel sorry for Billy? How has Barry Hines made you feel that way?

3 'Hines is a champion of the working class.' Do you agree?

A Taste of Honey

1 Write character descriptions of everyone in the play. Whom do you think is the best drawn character?

2 What evidence is there that this play is written by a woman?

3 'What happens to Jo is entirely the fault of Helen.' Do you agree?

Cider with Rosie

1 Give the impression you have gained of Laurie Lee's mother from your reading of Cider With Rosie, referring to some incidents in detail.

2 'The last days of my childhood were also the last days of the village.' How well does Laurie Lee make you aware of the way of life that is coming to an end?

3 'Granny Trill and Granny Walton were rival ancients and lived on one another's nerves.' Show how the account of these two old ladies with its humour and its sadness adds interest to Cider With Rosie.

Gregory's Girl

1 Show how the author understands teenagers.

2 How does the play reflect life in a comprehensive school? Could it have been more real?

3 How is humour used in the play? Mention some of the humorous situations. Do we laugh at or with Gregory? What language do you find amusing?

Animal Farm

1 Write an account of the emergence of the pigs as rulers. What is the significance of this in terms of human society?

2 Is *Animal Farm* an entirely sad story? Give reasons for your answers.

3 Give an account of the building of the windmill showing how the idea came into being and how all the efforts of the animals were eventually frustrated.

Spring and Port Wine

1 How has the author made you feel that this is a real family?

2 Write the letter Hilda writes to an 'agony aunt' about what happened. Also write the aunt's reply.

3 Write character descriptions of Rafe and Daisy. How would you describe their marriage?

Hobson's Choice

1 'This play is not really about a shoe shop. It could have had many other settings.' Discuss this statement.

2 Write character studies of all the women in the play.

3 What are the qualities that have made *Hobson's Choice* a classic comedy? Why is it still relevant today?

An Inspector Calls

1 Give evidence to show that J. B. Priestley feels deeply about the injustices suffered by the working class.

2 How might Priestley's play still have a message for us today? 'Nobody in his senses goes to the theatre to be told what to think,' wrote Priestley. Is Priestley trying to make you think like he does?

3 'There is far too much coincidence in this play.' Write a defence of Priestley's use of coincidence.

Z for Zachariah

1 Write a letter to the heads of government in America and Russia telling them to read this book and pointing out what they might learn from it.

2 What are the worst aspects of the nuclear winter the book describes.

3 Write full character descriptions of Ann and Loomis.

The Stories of Roald Dahl

1 How does Roald Dahl create suspense in his stories? Give examples from these and any of the stories you have seen on the television.

2 Write about the characters you find most interesting in these stories. Do you find any of them not like real-life characters?

3 Dahl has been attacked as being unsuitable as a writer for children and teenagers. Write in his defence saying what is particularly entertaining in his work. You may also refer briefly to any of his children's stories you have read.

Acknowledgements

We are grateful to the following for permission to reproduce photographs: BBC Enterprises, pages 156 and 157; British Film Institute, pages 85 and 92 above; Camera Press, page 132 (photo L'Express/Jean-Regis Roustan); Frank Lane Agency, page 105 (photo Leonard Lee Rue) and 113 (photo Arthur Christiansen); Ronald Grant Archive, pages 5, 11, 27, 34, 35, 36 above (all United Artists), 53, 77, 81 below (all ITC), 119, 123, 127, 128 above (all EMI/Warner Brothers), 131, 134, 139, 140, 141 and 151 (all ITC); Sally and Richard Greenhill, page 153; Greenwich Theatre, page 149; ITC, pages 39 and 52; Kobal Collection, pages 81 above (ITC), and 92 below (British Film Institute); Laurie Lee, pages 55, 61, 64, 67, and 71; Network Photographers, page 155 (photo Steve Benbow); Catherine Shakespeare Lane, pages 163, 169 and 171; United Artists Corporation, pages 19 and 36 below; John Vickers Archives, page 148; Warner Brothers, page 128 below.

Illustrations by:
Tessa Hamilton, pages 7 and 8
Edward McLachlan, page 110

Series designed by Jenny Palmer of Pentaprism

We are grateful to the following for permission to reproduce copyright material:

the author, John Agard for his poem 'Palm Tree King' from *Mangoes and Bullets*; the author's agent for extracts from pp 7–8, 17–18, 23, 47–48 *A Taste of Honey* by Shelagh Delaney Copyright © 1958 by Shelagh Delaney (pub Methuen Inc); Faber and Faber Ltd for the poems 'Making Cocoa for Kingsley Amis' and 'Reading Scheme' from pp 62 and 17 *Making Cocoa for Kingsley Amis* by Wendy Cope and the poem 'Warty Bliggens the Toad' from *Archie and Mehitabel* by Don Marquis; the author's agents for an extract from the play *Animal Farm*, Peter Hall's version of the book by George Orwell © Peter Hall; William Heinemann Ltd for extracts from pp 208–210 *Of Mice and Men and Cannery Row* and pp 168–172 *The Grapes of Wrath* by John Steinbeck; The Marvell Press for the poem 'Wires' from p 27 *The Less Deceived* by Philip Larkin; John Murray (Publishers) Ltd for the poem 'False Security' from *Collected Poems* by John Betjeman; Penguin Books Ltd for the poem 'Hugger Mugger' from pp 36–38 *Hot Dog and Other Poems* by Kit Wright (Kestrel Books, 1981), Copyright © Kit Wright, 1981; James McGibbon as Stevie Smith's Literary Executor for the poem 'Emily Writes Such a Good Letter' from *The Complete Poems of Stevie Smith* (Penguin Modern Classics); the author's agents for an extract from pp 103–107 *There is a Happy Land* by Keith Waterhouse (pub Longman Imprint Books).

We have been unable to trace the copyright holder in the poem 'The Rebel' by Mari Evans from p 58 *Sounds and Silences* and would appreciate any information that would enable us to do so.